King of the Wild Suburb

A memoir of fathers, sons and guns

Michael A. Messner

Plain View Press
P.O. 42255
Austin, TX 78704

plainviewpress.net
pk@plainviewpress.net
512-441-2452

Copyright © 2011 Michael A. Messner. All rights reserved under International and Pan-American Copyright Conventions. No part of this book may be reproduced or distributed in any form or by any means, or stored in a data base or retrieval system, without written permission from the author. All rights, including electronic, are reserved by the author and publisher.

ISBN: 978-1-935514-90-9
Library of Congress Number: 2011926109

Cover art: Photo by Fred A. Raab
Cover design by Pam Knight

Also by Michael A. Messner

It's All For the Kids: Gender, Families and Youth Sports
Out of Play: Critical Essays on Gender and Sport
Taking the Field: Women, Men, and Sports
Politics of Masculinities: Men in Movements
Sex, Violence and Power in Sports: Rethinking Masculinity
Power at Play: Sports and the Problem of Masculinity

Edited Volumes
Gender Through the Prism of Difference
Men's Lives
Paradoxes of Youth and Sport
Masculinities, Gender Relations, and Sport
Sport, Men and the Gender Order: Critical Feminist Perspectives

For my family

Contents

Prologue: The Last Hunt	9
1 The Young Prince	13
2 With the Men	23
3 Gramps' Den	33
4 Guns	45
5 A Boy and His Dog	57
6 Stout-Hearted Men	73
7 Trophy Head	97
8 Heroic noses	105
9 La Brea Tar Pits	115
10 Tall Tales	129
Epilogue: Hunting for Each Other	147
Author's Note	151
About the Author	153

Mr. Roosevelt, when are you going to get beyond the boyishness of killing things?
    John Muir, to Teddy Roosevelt, 1903

For it is not in giving life but in risking life that man is raised above the animal; that is why superiority has been accorded in humanity not to the sex that brings forth but to that which kills.
    Simone de Beauvoir, 1949

"Why do you hunt and fish?" I'm often asked. The easiest answer is: "My father and all my ancestors did it before me."
    Jimmy Carter, 1996

Prologue: The Last Hunt

The last time I went hunting with my dad, I didn't carry a rifle. A few years earlier, I'd realized that I hated killing animals. Now in college and living away from home, I'd come to associate deer hunting with the Vietnam War culture that I'd turned so virulently against. The Beatles seemed to speak to me when they sang, "Hey Bungalow Bill, What did you kill, Bungalow Bill?" But on some other plane of consciousness, somewhere deeper than my political views, I still knew that neither Dad nor Gramps was the crass, trophy-hunting "All American bullet-headed Saxon Mother's son" mocked by John Lennon's dripping sarcasm. I'd hunted with Dad and Gramps since I was a seven-year old boy. I knew they approached the activity safely and with an ethical reverence for the animals they hunted. And I knew that hunting was the main way Gramps connected, father-to-son, with Dad; and they, eventually, with me.

But this was 1973, and I had now denounced hunting—at least to my friends at college—as a violent proto-military activity through which men bonded with each other, excluded women, and subjugated nature. Hunting was part of everything that was wrong with the world, everything I was fighting to change.

Nevertheless, here I was, a twenty-one year old commie peacenik, my long hair tied back with a paisley headband, coaxing my beat-up powder-blue Corolla with the "Question Authority" bumper sticker two hundred miles south in the scorching August sun of the Sacramento Valley, to hang out with a bunch of short-haired middle-aged Nixon-loving gun-toting men.

Dad had phoned a couple of weeks earlier to invite me to join him at his new hunting club near Los Banos. His voice sounded thin, uncharacteristically tentative on the other end of the line.

"I figure it's been what, three or four years, Mike? Why don't you drive down for the weekend? I can bring your rifle."

I wasn't so sure about this.

"Will Gramps be there?"

"No, Gramps had to give it up a couple of years ago. He's seventy-seven now, you know."

That was the kicker, picturing Dad hunting without Gramps.

"Okay," I said, my voice likely conveying my mixed feelings.

As soon as I hung up, I decided I would go, but I would honor the secret promise I had made eight years earlier never again to shoot a deer. And this time, I would not hold to this vow through subterfuge. This time I would do it straight up, publicly, by not carrying a gun.

This had seemed a noble idea in the comfortable privacy of my college apartment the night I hung up the phone with my dad. But now, as I shot down the arrow-straight stretch of I-5, my cassette player blasting Derek and the Dominos, Clapton's guitar lacerating the hot air buffeting through my open windows, a knot of worry swelled in my stomach. How would Dad react to my decision to join the hunt with no rifle? This would be awkward, at the very least. I didn't expect Dad to be pissed at me; worse, I feared I'd embarrass him in front of his longtime hunting friend Bob Shackelford, not to mention the guys I'd never met in his new hunting club. I doubted that anybody had ever walked a hunt unarmed with those guys.

As my car tires ground to a halt on the rocky dirt road of the campsite, I dropped the volume on my stereo. Through my bug-splattered windshield I spied Dad and Bob laughing with two burly men as they unloaded sleeping bags, coolers and rifles from their jeeps and pickup trucks. And I wondered, not for the last time: What in the hell am I doing here?

○

Over the past four decades, starting in my college years, I have been preoccupied with the question, "What is manhood?" Inspired by feminism, I have interrogated my own life, and the broader social world around me, wondering how it is that men commit so many horrible acts of violence against women, against other men, against ourselves, and indeed, against the natural world. In my teaching, public lectures and books about boys and men, I have rejected the simplistic but popular idea that males are naturally hard-wired to dominate others—that "all that testosterone" predisposes us, like the positive ends of two magnets, to repel away from human intimacy, and to be drawn instead to guns and violence. Instead, I ask different questions about boys and men: How does our immersion in cultures of domination and violence distort our humanity? How do we nevertheless manage to connect with each other, to find and express love and intimacy with others?

A boy's developing sense of masculinity is insecure and tentative, and most of us learn early on to hide our self-doubts beneath a veneer of bravado. I know I did. As a young boy, I was very aware of the daily risks to my fragile sense of self, as I watched other boys and men routinely suffer humiliation—or worse—for showing any sign of vulnerability or weakness. I learned from the adult men around me, and through a succession of popular culture images of male heroism—Davy Crockett, John Wayne, John Glenn and Willie Mays among them—that the world promised to heap status, glory and love upon me if I grew up to be tough, if I suppressed my empathy for others, and especially if I became a winner. I swallowed this idea of male heroism hook, line, and sinker.

When boys like me buy into the myth of male heroism, what happens to our very human needs for connection, intimacy, and love? After we shut boys down emotionally, after we scare the crap out of them with the knowledge that it is grown-up boys who fight and die in wars, after we convince them they will be viewed as failures if they lose in the competitive marketplace of manly success, what kinds of ways do we offer these boys to connect with others? What situations do we put them in, and what kinds of opportunities do those situations offer them to experience closeness with others?

For Gramps and Dad, hunting provided this means of connection. When Dad was a boy, Gramps took him hunting several times a year to Lake County in Northern California. These and imagined future hunting trips became the foundation of their relationship, and a major subject of the letters they exchanged when Dad was in the South Pacific during World War II. During the decades following the war, Dad returned the favor by taking Gramps hunting, until Gramps was too old to continue. These hunts made them the best of pals for life.

By the time I was seven, Gramps and Dad had placed a rifle in my hands, and had begun to initiate me into a men-only world of hunting for quail, pheasant, and especially deer. Hunting worked well for Gramps and Dad;

ultimately, it did not work so well for me. By the end of my teen years, I had decided to lay down my rifle, and had taken a path to manhood that I saw as very different from the roads taken by Gramps and Dad. But in rejecting hunting, I was letting go of an emotionally salient lifeline that had been extended to me, from my grandfather through my father. Years after Dad's and Gramps' deaths, I continue to poke at the scars left by this self-imposed wound. And I wonder: what kind of a father am I? I have offered my two sons a different model of manhood. Is it better?

○

The day of the hunt, I tromped loudly down the bottom of the ravine, flanked on the left and right ridges by several armed men. With no rifle in my hands, my usefulness on this hunt was essentially to play the role of a dog, fighting blindly through thick shrubs and brush, hoping to flush out a buck for the men. We didn't see a single deer that day, and as we returned to camp and started preparing dinner, I wondered again if I'd embarrassed Dad, showing up from college with my long hair and my bizarre insistence on walking a hunt unarmed. Maybe I shouldn't have come at all. Dad, who would die four years later, walked up and handed me a can of Burgie, still dripping chips of ice from the cooler. We each took a welcome slug of the cold beer. And he said, "Thanks for coming, Pal."

After the group polished off a dinner that included an industrial-sized vat of delicious rigatoni, Dad passed a bota bag to me, and showed me how to extend my arms fully as red wine streamed directly into my mouth. Later that evening under stars made opaque by hissing Coleman lanterns, one of the guys took up his accordion, and played an upbeat Italian tune. Dad, clad only in his white boxers, a tucked-in white T-shirt and a smile, climbed on top of his cot and performed a graceful tango as all of us exploded into laughter and cheered him on.

1
The Young Prince

"Wake up! Wake up! It's happened! The new Prince is born!"

I sit spellbound in the El Rey Theatre, a four-year-old boy in 1956, nestled between my sisters and my mother. A half-eaten package of Milk Duds rests forgotten in my lap. Five minutes into the film, I am mesmerized by a story that resonates deeply, echoing already-familiar Biblical themes: Bambi is like Jesus in his crèche, asleep next to Mary, as the Three Kings and others pay homage and share in the collective effervescence of the Good News. Something even more personal resonates: *The father.* I wonder: *Where is the father?* As the animals of the forest leave the newly christened Bambi resting with his mother, the view pans out and then up…up to the ridge above the thicket. Now, we see him. There he is: erect, perfectly still, his muscular body and antlered head silhouetted against the sky. Separate from his family, the Father stands aloof from the celebration in the thicket. Above, he watches, listens and protects.

O

For years before I was born, I was already Mike. It was part of the plan that my parents would have a son, and my mom knew she'd call this boy Mike. On a shelf next to my desk sits a steel piggy bank, not much larger than a baseball. The pig's left ear is bent, and most of the silver plating has chipped and peeled off of the mottled surface of the pig's body. If you look closely, near the coin-slot on the pig's back, "Mike's" is engraved in large,

Edwardian script. This piggy bank had preceded me, waiting years for me to be born. And I've always wondered: has this bank always belonged to me, or had another boy, a stillborn or miscarried brother, also pre-named Mike, owned it before me? Not long ago, I asked my mom about the bank, and she replied on e-mail.

All my life I had planned on having a little boy of my own and calling him Mike. Lost so many babies in between Terry, Melinda and you and finally when I had a boy there you were. Two good friends of mine from where I was working in Oakland gave me the piggy bank when I was preg. with Terry and I kept it all those years waiting for my Mike…You were caesarian and of course I did not know what I was having till I came to and your darling Dad sat there and told me it was another girl…which would have been ok but I could tell by the big smile on his face that it was finally you…then the nurse could not stand it any more and she said…no you had a boy…what a thrill and what happiness for both of us…I am so glad we kept trying, even tho there were heartaches in between.

It's as though I'd existed already for so long in my parents' imaginations, all that was needed to make it real was the minor detail of my successfully achieving corporeal form: "There you were…It was finally you." By the time I was old enough to pee standing up, I was already aware that I was special, that my arrival had completed the picture for my parents. Toddler photos show me wearing a red fireman's outfit or sporting cowboy boots and holstered sixguns. As a three-year-old, dressing like Davy Crockett made me feel like a hero, and it also clearly differentiated me from my older sisters, Terry and Linda. But I didn't really have to work too hard to accomplish this differentiation. I was a boy. No, I was *the* boy, the long-awaited boy, The Young Prince.

After Mom birthed two daughters, clustered around several terrible miscarriages, Dr. Nunes told her it would be dangerous to chance another pregnancy. But she wanted desperately to try one last time to have the son she and Dad had hoped for. Gramps sweetened the pot by offering Mom her choice—a fur coat or a mangle—if she delivered a grandson. It worked; I arrived July 1, 1952, via Caesarian section. Her brief career as a fashion model now well behind her, Mom chose the mangle. We were the only family I knew who owned one of these hulking ironing machines. Mom would regularly roll it into the center of our kitchen, where it sat proudly like a post-war wife's Rolls Royce. I was prohibited from touching it, for fear that I would scald myself or, worse, smash my tiny fingers between its heated rotating cylinders. I loved the warm smell of freshly-pressed sheets rolling out of Mom's mangle, but it always made me wonder: If another daughter had turned up instead of me, would the family have had to sleep on wrinkled sheets?

Mom was always there. Always cooking, doing laundry, ironing, reading stories, taking us to the movies, putting us to bed with a song and a prayer. Immersed in her love, I once asked her to wait for me, so I could marry her when I grew up. Where Dad presumably fit in to this plan, I hadn't fully thought through. Mom smiled and said yes, she would wait for me.

Mom was adept at waiting for Dad. He was regularly away—at basketball practice, in Oakland with the Naval Reserve, deer hunting with Gramps for the weekend. Dad's absences burdened Mom. On his triumphant returns home—bearing another coach-of-the-year trophy, another promotion with the Navy, another dead buck with which we kids would pose for pictures on the front lawn—Mom would clap and lead us in cheers, "Yayyyy! Daddy's home!"

When Dad brought the stuffed buck Joe home and mounted him on the wall above my bed, I was awed by his majesty. With a great sense of reverence, I bestowed what felt to me the highest honor on Mom, telling her that when she died, I would have her stuffed, so I could keep her forever mounted on the wall of my home. Amused, Mom submitted this story to *Readers Digest*, where it was summarily rejected as perhaps too macabre a twist on the 1950's Oedipal dance.

○

Watching Bambi in the El Rey Theatre—one of my first clear memories—was heartwarming, frightening and confusing. My father went away to the mountains and brought home stuffed deer heads for the wall, and venison for the barbeque. In Disney's film, the hunters were the evil interlopers whose terrible violence threatened an entire world of lovable forest creatures. To my four-year-old eyes, Bambi was not meat; his family seemed to mirror my own. One scene mesmerized me: Several bucks appear suddenly in the meadow, sparring and running about. Seated in the theatre, I witness the exciting mystery of this public life of men as an outsider, with much the same awe that Bambi seems to feel. Without warning, the Father appears: regal, pausing momentarily, frozen in place like a statue, then moving very slowly from the forest, striding across the meadow right past Bambi, glancing briefly over his shoulder at the fawn after he passes—aloof,

Michael A. Messner

Linny, me, Mom and Terry (1954).

without uttering a word. Bambi looks at him hopefully, then shrinks back, confused, possibly ashamed. Mother steps up and Bambi whispers, "He stopped and looked at me."

She translates the silent Father for Bambi, "Yes, I know."

Bambi asks, "Why was everyone still, when he came on the meadow?"

"Everyone respects him," Mother replies. "He's very brave, and very wise. That's why he's known as The Great Prince of the Forest."

She says this as the Father walks away slowly into the woods, pausing on a high vantage point to gaze about, alert for danger, literally above it all.

Like Bambi, I watched carefully as I got glimpses of my father in his public life—respected high school basketball coach, former college football player, Naval officer—and I relished seeing him through the eyes of others. Once, when I went to Oakland for a weekend with Dad, I admired how he carried himself as he moved about the Navy base in his uniform. I loved to witness the moments when enlisted men and lower-ranked officers snapped to attention as The Commander, my Dad, walked by. Dad returned their snappy salutes with a casual but authoritative style.

At the basketball games in a packed gym, Dad orchestrated the boys on the court. He won games, championships, coach-of the year awards, and was lauded in the *Salinas Californian* as the most respected coach in the Coast Counties Athletic League. When I was about seven, I became Dad's assistant. I sat next to him on the bench during games and on school busses when the team traveled to Montcrey, Watsonville or Santa Cruz. Dad put me in charge of providing towels to the players during time-outs—dry ones to wipe off the sweat; water-soaked ones for the boys to suck on—as Dad instructed the team in pick-and-rolls and man-to-man defense. During warm-ups as the band played, the pom-pom girls danced, and the building buzzed with anticipation, I stood proudly below the basket and retrieved balls for the players, stepping finally on to the playing court to collect the balls as the buzzer sounded. Little in my life before or since ever felt so good as when I was Dad's towel boy.

Watching Dad and his basketball team I learned how to act when hurt. If you sprained an ankle, you should "try to walk it off." When you jammed or dislocated a finger, you had to "shake it off." If the sprain, jam or dislocation was severe enough, then Coach Messner himself wrapped the injured appendage with his roll of two-inch wide surgical tape—the stuff that smelled like the white paste kindergarteners ate. If you lost some skin on the floor, and especially if it left you bleeding, Dad would observe clinically, "You've really got a good one there." Then he'd smear some Basiquent on the wound, and cover it with a bandage. The lesson was obvious: Don't whine; wrap it, put Basiquent on it, shake it off, and go play.

One summer day when I was eight, I was racing my red Schwinn around the block with two other boys. In the lead, speeding down the middle of the street and approaching the busy intersection of San Antonio and Acacia, I decided it was prudent to hop the curb. I'd done this a million times. Take it at a soft angle, and your bike slides right up and over. This time I missed it. Before I knew it, I was flying through the air, over my handlebars, and landing face-first on the sidewalk. As I lay dazed and bleeding, one of my friends ran to get my mom, two houses away, who promptly hustled me home and right into the car.

"Wait here," Mom said, as she ran into the house to get me a towel. I snuck a peek of myself in the visor mirror and was horrified: broken front teeth, lacerated and swelling lips, blood dripping from my chin.

Mom somehow got me to the office of Dr. Baughn, our dentist. All of the kids called him "Butcher Baughn," due to the sadistic pleasure he seemed to take in inflicting pain on kids. As you sat in one of his dental chairs, your terror would build with every *screek—screek—screeek* of Butcher Baughn's rubber-soled shoes on the polished linoleum floor as he bustled from room-to-room, simultaneously torturing three kids. One of his favorite things to say was, "Oh, I don't think we'll need Novocaine for this one," as he revved up his power drill right in your face, in much the same way that a teenaged motorcyclist would gun his engine in anticipation of blowing you off at the intersection when the light turns green.

As the nurse hustled Mom and I in the Butcher tossed a kid out of his chair to make room for me. I sat down and I noticed out of the corner of my eye Butcher Baughn and the nurse lunging to catch my fainting mom. As they sat her down, I wisecracked, "Oh, I guess now I'll have to take care of *her!*"

Back home, I lay stitched up on my bed, wondering what it'd feel like when the Novocaine wore off. Mom soothed me, stroking my forehead and hair, and asked "Is there anything I can get you? Anything you need, Honey?"

"Dad," I responded instantly.

And it wasn't because I expected him to drive the 100 miles back from the Oakland Naval Air Station to stroke my hair and commiserate with me. What I really wanted was to hear him say, "You really got a good one there," and see how very brave I was.

○

Two weeks after I was born, my father hand-wrote a letter to his parents, postmarked July 14, 1952.

Sun Nite

Dearest Mom and Dad:

Well, we have all of our family in bed and sound asleep—hope they stay that way all nite. Fed Mike after you left & he took 4 oz.'s. He stayed awake till about 8 o'clock, watched the kids eat dinner from the drain board & was good as gold. MaMa & I played two games of Old Maid with Terry & put her to bed.

I wanted to write you both just a few lines tonite to let you know how much Anita & I appreciate all that you have done for us. It seems rather inadequate to say "Thanks" after you spend such a week with us, & then on top of it all you give us such a wonderful gift. We have never been a very emotional or demonstrative family, so I thot maybe I could do a better job of thanking you both by writing a few lines. Of course Anita was thrilled beyond words with the mangle, but the greatest thrill for her—as she told me tonite after you left—was the realization that you both thought enough of her to do so much for her—that is, caring for her and her baby the way you did all week Mom--& then the expensive gift on top of that. We are both very grateful & thankful that our children have such fine Grandparents & we have such fine parents. I only hope that we can do for, & give as much to, our children as you two have done.

As I grow older I realize more each day that one's children can cause their parents' greatest sadness & gladness. For my part, I know that this child has given his parents some heartaches & sadness but not wantonly so. Also I know there has been gladness—a good share--& now I believe there shall be abundance for our future. A future we want, & pray to share with you Mother & Dad for a good many, many years—God willing.

It's 10:15 & no sound from Mike as yet—he ate at 5:30. Here's hoping. I'll leave this for now and finish in the morning so I can tell you what kind of a nite I had. Nite for now & our love to you both—all 5 of us Wow!

Good Morning—and a good nite. Fed Mike at 11:15—he woke again at 2:10 AM, I gave him his bottle, burped him, changed him, and that's all I heard from him till 7:45 this AM. So you can stop worrying Granny, you have him well educated. He ate again at 11 O'clock (bath first of course) and is now sound asleep—Well have to go to town, so see you later —

All our love — Your Son

Michael A. Messner

Dad's 1952 letter to Gramps and Granny has a joyful kind of "finished deal" feel to it. Life, as it had been planned, could now commence. My arrival completed the blueprint, filled out the picture of the imagined postwar family. And my birth seemed to allow Gramps to take a deep breath of relief and satisfaction; the Messner name would now carry on. Gramps called Terry "Number One," in honor of her being the firstborn grandchild. Poor Linny was dubbed "Number Two." But I was never called "Number Three," because I was in a category all my own. Gramps' patrilineal passions ran deep, due in part to his continuing shame at having been born a bastard; the Messner name was his mother's. For Gramps, it was crucial for a man to pass on his name to a son, and in turn, that son to his son, and on and on. Twenty-five years later, a year after Dad's death, Gramps would impress this on me with a sudden burst of anger over the fact that I'd not yet produced another Messner. But for now, as a young boy I was content to bask in the knowledge that I was more than merely wanted, more than loved—I was an essential part of the plan. I completed things.

Gramps with Terry, me and Linny (circa 1955).

2
With the Men

"All buck hunters rise and shine!"

It was 4:30 a.m., dark and cold. I buried my head deeper in my warm mummy bag. As always, Dad was up first, dancing barefoot across the creaky cabin floor, pumping the Coleman lanterns, lighting the gas burners under the coffee pot, and cheerfully urging everyone to get up, get fed and out of here before sunrise.

"Let's go! Up and at 'em!" Dad-the-coach exhorted.

"Shut up Messner, dammit to Hell," Bones groaned as he sat up on his cot.

I dressed in my sleeping bag, then reluctantly dragged my shivering body to the table and huddled over steaming scrambled eggs and hot chocolate.

As everyone piled into two jeeps and headed up the mountain, I took my spot on the hood of our jeep, where Dad had asked me to sit to distribute the weight more evenly on the front tires. I felt heroic, perched like a military hood ornament, one hand cradling my rifle, the other gripping the tow-bar, feet on the bumper, eyes peeled for deer.

Once when I was eleven years old, just as dawn was breaking, I rode shotgun and as the jeep's tires ground around a bend in the rocky dirt road, Dad stopped suddenly. Frozen in our headlights, not thirty feet away and staring at us, a mountain lion paused, the hindquarters of a freshly killed fawn dangling from its jaws. Dad tooted the jeep's horn, and the startled lion dropped its catch in the road and darted into the brush.

"Go get it, Mike," Dad told me.

I climbed down, shot a nervous glance at the spot where the lion had disappeared, snagged the still-warm hindquarters, and put it in the back of the jeep. That night, we ate venison that tasted like veal. There was no chest thumping about this among the men, but to me, this was unbelievably cool: we're eating meat we took from a lion!

○

From the late 1950's through the end of the 1960's Dad and Gramps belonged to a hunting club that consisted of the two of them and four other guys: Dad's close friend Bob Shackelford (whose son Duffy occasionally tagged along, like me), two brothers—Charley and Clarence Dake, and a character nicknamed Bones (a doctor of sorts: he managed a liquor store). For the weekends of deer season, these guys paid an aging furrowed rancher named Mr. Olds—a moniker that appealed to whatever sense of irony an eight-year old boy could muster—for access to his top country of rocky ravines and scrub brush in Chualar Canyon, about ten miles south of Salinas.

We crowded into a little cabin with peeling green paint, with an open front porch, a kitchen with a gas stove, and a cramped, screened sleeping porch with eight squeaky-springed cots. The kitchen décor was purely utilitarian: dishes, cups and flatware stacked on a shelf; pots and pans hanging from rusty nails in the wall. On the other side of the kitchen, a table covered with a vinyl tablecloth, surrounded by wobbly wood benches, served as the eating area. A cartoon, torn from a magazine and framed on the wall, was the room's most popular piece of art: A hunter is squatting with his pants at his ankles, propping himself up by grasping a clump of brush on his left, and his rifle on his right; behind the brush, two men dressed in full hunting gear pause, rifles at full alert, and one says, "Listen! I think I heard a buck snort!"

Chualar Canyon in August and September was a dry, blisteringly hot place, especially if you were hiking through eye-high sagebrush in the late-morning hours. Bits of brush would stick to your sweaty flesh and end up inside your clothes—somehow even inside your underwear. Getting a buck was a rare event; heck, even seeing a deer was a rare event.

Dad used to sing this World War II Navy song that went, "I joined the Navy to see the world; but what did I see? I saw the sea."

The little green cabin in Chualar Canyon (Circa 1967).

I came to think of Chualar Canyon similarly: I went hunting to get a deer, but what did I get? Sagebrush down my pants, and poison oak on my balls. We rarely saw a deer, and if we did, it usually was not a buck. Oh, we saw "sign" of deer; in fact, it was only the occasional sighting of track or what Dad jokingly called "coffee beans" that gave evidence that deer indeed inhabited what felt to me like unlivable terrain.

Places on the Olds' property had mysterious or incongruous names that the men used as shorthand for various hunts, as in "Tomorrow, we'll hunt The Frenchman," which was a ravine that included the remains of a crumbling stone wall, legendarily erected by the Chinese after they were done building the railroad. Why the Chinese had come to this out-of-the-way place to build a wall was never explained, nor was the connection between a Chinese wall and a Frenchman. Near the top of the Olds' property was Nick's Cabin, a crumbled foundation with a few bits of rotting wood scattered about. It had never been completed, the men said, due to something tragic having happened to Mr. Olds' son Nick.

I loved The Esterbrook Flats—a meadow brown-dry in the late summer, with a scatter of mature California Oaks. Where the name Esterbrook came from was anybody's guess, but for sure it was flat. This was not a place to hunt; rather, it was a calm resting place with some rare shade, where the men would drink from their canteens and strategize about the hunt. Once, after a fruitless early morning hunt, the men left Duffy and me at the Flats for an hour or two while they pursued one more hunt before lunch. Armed with Duffy's pellet gun, we shot at and missed a couple of tweety birds in the trees. When we saw a brown tarantula the size of my hand crabbing its way across a pile of dirt a few feet from us, Duffy shot it, the impact sending the giant arachnid tumbling directly at us. We screamed in terror and ran for it. Safely at a distance, our hearts still pounding with excitement, Duffy upped the ante by reminding me that the week before, the men had killed two young wild pigs near the Esterbrook Flats. What if the pigs' furious parent showed up right now, tusks raging, bent on revenge? Duffy said he was a good shot and would put a pellet right in the wild boar's eye. I said I thought that might just make it mad. Suddenly, in the absence of the men and their jeeps, the quiet Esterbrook Flats felt menacing. When the men returned, Duffy and I were sitting high in the safety of an oak tree, giggling nervously about three hundred pound wild boars.

Following the morning hunt, lunchtime at the cabin was the best. We'd eat baloney sandwiches and chips, and guzzle cans of ice-cold Shasta Cola. Occasionally we'd nap, but more often Duffy and I would go down to the muddy trickle of a stream below the cabin to catch minnows and long-legged water striders. Other times, we'd sit on the porch of the cabin with our rifles, pick a rock or a stump far up the facing mountain, and shoot at it for target practice. When Duffy and I had to pee, we'd launch two ten-foot arcs right from the edge of the porch, and the men would laugh and marvel at the youthful pressure we could muster.

Once, Dad stood twenty paces from the back of the cabin, peeing in the dirt, and Bob yelled, "Hey, Russell! What's that you're holding in your hand?"

Dad responded with no hesitation: "Not much."

My chest filled with admiration at the eloquence of this response. I made a mental note to remember that one, just in case somebody ever asked me the same question. It was pretty obvious that it was an honor to be here with my dad and these men.

○

Every hunting weekend was a ritualized series of events. Friday afternoon after school, Dad, Gramps and I would pack our sleeping bags, clothes, guns, and a cooler full of food and drinks into the gray 1947 Willys jeep that Gramps had bought for this very purpose. We'd squeeze into the jeep's tiny cab, and plug south on Highway 101 at no better than 45 miles per hour through the heart of the Salinas Valley's ploughed lettuce and celery fields. Ten miles later, at the sleepy little town of Chualar, we'd bend east into the hills, and before long, we'd be kicking up dust on rutted dirt roads, stopping occasionally to open padlocked private gates, and eventually arrive at the cabin.

Dad always took charge of the dinner barbeque: steaks on Friday, chicken on Saturday, with juicy venison sausage both nights. Bones insisted that we needed no green vegetables, because, he argued, "chili beans are vegetables."

This must have been a convincing argument, because we had chili beans with every dinner. Gramps had charge of the kitchen, and always cooked up his famous raw fries—thickly sliced potatoes fried with onions in plenty of bacon grease. I relished sprinting from the outdoor barbeque that lay in the mostly dry creek bed gully, up the steep path to the cabin, where I would deliver a slice of steaming sausage to Gramps. In turn, he would let me taste his delicious bacon-soaked delicacy, and occasionally, he'd give me a lesson in something useful, like how to drink with one arm directly from a gallon jug of root beer.

The men drank, too: whiskey or beer as they stood around the smoking barbeque, and red wine with the meal. But they kept a strict rule that one never drank during the day, before or during a hunt. A couple of years before, they'd kicked a guy named Dick out of the club because he carried a cooler of beer in his jeep while hunting. I also heard them gripe about how he brought his wife along a couple of times (to me, this tall blonde woman with a rifle was glamorously incongruous), but the men claimed it was the beer, not the wife, that led to Dick's expulsion.

After dinner, the men would sit around the table and plan the next morning's hunt like a carefully choreographed military operation. As I watched and listened, I imagined General Patton mapping the minutiae of tactical moves in the hedgerows of Normandy. I marveled at how over the course of a full deer season, the men's strategies regularly yielded for each his two-buck limit, even in the stingy terrain of Chualar Canyon.

When the battle plan had been settled, it was early bedtime for the two boys. Duffy and I were torn: we wanted to get to sleep quickly, to avoid being kept awake by the men's deafening chorus of snoring to the beat of bean-fueled percussive flatulence. Gramps' buzz saw snoring was virtuoso: He soloed over everyone else's rhythm. But Duffy's and my goal of quickly getting to sleep was eclipsed by the forbidden thrill of eavesdropping on snippets of the men's conversations, which we could easily hear through the thin wall that divided the sleeping porch and the kitchen.

One night, as Duffy and I lay awake, Bones loudly proclaimed about his wife, "I hope when I get home that I don't find Margaret exactly as I left her."

"How's that?" one of the men asked.

"Freshly fucked."

This was greeted with a burst of raucous laughter, followed by Bob's, "Sshhhh! The boys!"

Other times, we'd hear Bob and Dad talking in hushed tones, their voices rising just enough for us to hear that they were discussing their kids, their wives, their work, their lives. One thing Duffy and I did not want to hear the men say was, "Tomorrow morning, how about we hunt The Olive Trees?"

Whoever named this place "The Olive Trees" must have been a practical joker. There were almost no trees at all, much less olive trees. It was simply a steep, heat-blasted mountain covered with dry sagebrush and impenetrable splashes of red-barked manzanita. There were only two temperatures

The cabin's kitchen was Gramps' realm (1967).

in this place—bone-chilling cold and blistering hot. As we arrived at the base of the mountain at dawn, I trembled, frozen to the bone, despite my layered hooded sweatshirt over a long-sleeved flannel shirt and a t-shirt. Dad would always suggest that I leave the sweatshirt in the jeep.

"No thanks," I shivered.

We strapped our rifles to our backs and began to climb straight to the top, where we hoped to find deer. Five minutes into our ascent, the sun rising at our backs, I was sweating bullets, the now-useless sweatshirt tied around my waist.

I dreaded this climb. Halfway up, puffing and sweating, I could always count on Dad letting me grab on to his belt, to tow me for a ways. This service came with a price: at some point, Dad would cut loose with one of his patented three-tone farts. I admired Dad's tonality, but gasping for air at his butt-level made the Olive Trees hunt an even more dismal place.

Despite the heat, I'd have to keep the flannel shirt on, buttoned at the wrists, to avoid poison oak and ticks. Ticks, Dad had told me, hung on the tips of dry brush, waiting for a warm mammal like me. Once, back at the cabin during dinner, my fingers found a soft bulb stuck to the base of my skull, just above the back of my neck. Dad inspected it and declared that I'd become host to a tick, its abdomen swollen with my blood like a miniature water balloon. Gramps and Dad held a short debate about how to get it off me. Dad argued that if you twist it a quarter-turn, counter-clockwise, it would pull its own head out. Gramps disagreed.

"Nope, if you do that, you'll break its head off." He held up his lit cigarette: "You gotta burn its rear-end with this, and it'll pull out on its own."

Dad somehow won the debate, grabbed the tick and twisted.

"Oh, shoot," he said as the tick popped, covering his fingertips with my blood.

Three days later, I perched on Dr. Nunes' table as he scraped the remains of the tick from my infected wound, leaving a small white scar that shined like a crescent moon after each buzzed crew cut I'd get from Mom.

I hated that Olive Trees hunt. But fortunately, I took something from this place besides a scar on my head. I was eight years old the first time I walked this hunt with Dad, and less than halfway up the mountain, hot and dispirited, I nearly broke into tears. Looking up at the distant mountaintop, I told Dad, "I don't think I can make it."

Dad pointed to a stand of manzanita, thirty feet above us. "See that? Let's just walk to there."

We trudged to that spot and stopped, puffing. Dad took out his canteen, and handed it to me: "Just a sip."

The smooth metallic taste was wonderful. Putting the canteen back in his belt pouch, Dad pointed to a granite boulder, maybe another thirty feet up. "Let's walk to that rock."

At the rock, we stopped for a few breaths, and then he asked me, "Where should we walk next?"

I looked up: "That piece of brush," I said, and we walked up another short stretch of the mountain.

In that way, we made our way to the top, where Dad delivered no punch line, no moral-of-the-story, no take-home-lesson.

The Olive Trees hike became for me a potent metaphor for setting short-term goals toward a bigger goal that may otherwise seem daunting or even impossible. Two years later, I asked for a ten-speed bike, and Dad told me that if I saved up for it, he'd pay half. It took me six months: I washed cars and cut lawns and stacked the dollar bills one at a time in a cigar box in my bedroom. When I had twenty-four of them, Dad bought me a red Huffy Mark Ten at the Navy Exchange in Oakland, for $48. As a young man, after Dad's death, I spent eight years earning a Ph.D., jumping through one flaming hoop at a time. Now, as I sit writing, I could be overwhelmed with the mountain of memories and emotions that face me in trying to make sense of my life with Dad and Gramps. Instead, I write this part of the story. In a few minutes, I will walk to the kitchen and make myself a cold fruit smoothie. As I drink, I'll think about the next piece I'd like to write. Just focus on the next knoll, Dad taught me. Walk to it, pause for a breath. Look up; find a stand of manzanita, and head toward it.

3
Gramps' Den

A year after Dad died in 1977, I started graduate school, and moved to Oakland to live with Granny and Gramps for what turned out to be the last two years of Gramps' life. I can see now that they were both depressed, having recently endured their only son's death, and the precipitous decay of their aging bodies. I hoped my presence would help, and I guess it did a bit. But I really had no idea how to make life better for them.

Once a vibrant hub of family life, the house now seemed cavernous, nearly devoid of activity. I stuffed all my belongings into the smallest of three upstairs bedrooms. The others were musty museum pieces: the front room facing busy Claremont Avenue felt to me to be occupied by the ghost of my father; the corner bedroom by Aunt Minnie, a sweet retired nurse who during my childhood lived her final decade with Granny and Gramps. I had the entire upstairs to myself, but found comfort in my one little room. Surrounded by my books and records, I was insulated from my grandparents' sadness. By day, I attended seminars on social theory and research methods, and worked teaching smart Berkeley freshmen. By late afternoon, I was home with Granny and Gramps. I'd slug down two or three—sometimes four—cheap Lucky beers, and sit down to eat dinner with them. Granny didn't speak much; she'd retreated into a bewildered dementia, compounded by painkillers and sedatives. Gramps was 80, still sharp as a tack, but grumpy as hell. He rarely offered much in the way of sustained conversation.

Over dinner, Gramps sat in his dining chair, sipping his nightly glass of dark red burgundy, frequently choking and coughing up a clump of phlegm or half-chewed food into his napkin. Over the course of the meal, I tried to ignore the stack of gooey napkins he'd neatly pile between our two plates.

As Gramps ate, much of his face was hidden behind the trademark red visor—black with grime around the forehead—that he'd worn daily for the past decade. It kept the glare out of his eyes, he said. When my mom's second husband Harold tried to give Gramps a fresh white visor from Spreckels Sugar, where Harold worked, Gramps said "Thank you kindly," and put it on.

But by the next morning, the new hat was gone, and the cruddy red visor was firmly fixed on Gramps' head. He intended to die in it, I figured.

After washing the dishes and helping Granny and Gramps get to bed, I'd retreat to my upstairs room, close the door in relief, read a bit, and then get high and listen to music. Occasionally my fellow grad student Bill Solomon would join me in my upstairs sanctuary. Bill adored the Beatles, Karl Marx, basketball, and marijuana coupled with heaping mounds of ice cream. He and I, in other words, were fully compatible. We even looked alike: both tall, pushing thirty, bespectacled and bearded, one of our professors frequently mistook us for each other. Bill and I joked that one day we would secure a single professor job, split the work and the salary fifty-fifty, and nobody would be the wiser.

One Saturday night, Bill and I closed my bedroom door and settled in with a Thai stick I'd been told was shit-kicker stuff. Bill dropped the tone arm into the groove of John Mayall's *Memories*, and we toked up. It was indeed primo Thai: within minutes Bill and I were bereft of speech and zoned in to Mayall's melodic blues. That's when I heard the thump. I shot a glance at Bill, who was enjoying a rhythmic pitch-and-roll in my rocking chair.

"Did you hear a thump?" I asked.

"No…no I didn't hear anything," Bill murmured.

I decided to check it out. Downstairs I found Gramps flat on his back on the carpet next to Granny's bed.

"It's my hip. I think I busted it."

Indeed, Gramps' left leg looked normal, but his right foot bent to an unnatural ninety-degree angle. My heart rate quadrupled; I stood dumbfounded—stoned, speechless and fully flummoxed. It seemed to make sense to race upstairs and tell Bill.

"Bill," I hyperventilated, "Gramps fell; I think he broke his hip."

"Oh, bummer," he managed. "Anything I can do?"

I told him to wait there, and ran back down the steps.

By now, Granny was sitting up in bed crying and Gramps was getting mad. All I could think to do was to put a pillow under his head.

"Goddamn it Mike, call the Pastor."

"Right. Right," I said, "I'll go get him."

The Reverend Teachenor, my grandparents' Lutheran pastor, lived next door with his family. I sprinted next door to get him. He came right over and took charge, calmly assessing Gramps' condition, calling an ambulance, settling Granny down. I continued to be a pretty inept member of the emergency response team. As we waited for the ambulance, the pastor told me we needed a plan:

"One of us will need to go to the hospital with your grandfather, and one will need to stay here with your grandmother."

I pictured the nightmare of trying to drive to the hospital, and then navigating the bureaucratic procedures of emergency-room patient intake.

"I think I'll stay here with Granny."

After the ambulance left with Gramps, I sat with Granny for an hour or so, holding her hand and talking with her as she settled down and finally drifted off to sleep. Drained, I trudged upstairs, and opened the door to find Bill, still rocking in the free world, albeit now to a John Lennon album.

"Hey, Ace," he smiled with barely open eyes, "time for ice cream?"

☾

During the time I lived with them, Granny never once came upstairs, and after Gramps broke his hip, he never climbed the stairs again. He spent several weeks in the hospital and in physical therapy, and when he came home, each day I'd follow behind, spotting him as he plodded the downstairs loop behind his walker. I'd inch along behind, Gramps' few remaining wisps of thin white hair poking out of his visor, his rounded shoulders lurching under his flannel shirt as he lifted and dropped his walker. Emitting a nasal grunt with the effort of every step—"*Huh-huh; Huh-huh*"—Gramps herky-jerked down the narrow hallway toward the front-door foyer, his walker rising and then clunking on the linoleum, in rhythm with his grunts: "*Huh-huh*"; *Clunk*; "*Huh-huh*"; *Clunk*. We'd mark his daily progress by counting the number of times he could make the full loop from his hospital bed in the dining room, to the kitchen, down the narrow hallway to the foyer, back into the living room where we'd pass Granny in her hospital bed.

"Hi, Daddy," she'd wave as we passed.

"*Huh-huh*; Hi, Momma; *Huh-huh*"; *Clunk*. In the foyer, he'd sometimes pause to catch his breath, and gaze up the stairs.

Usually he said nothing, but once he asked me, in a whisper, "How's the den, my boy?"

"Uh—fine, I guess," I answered lamely.

In fact, these days I rarely ever set foot in the den. But that hadn't always been so.

Located upstairs in the turn-of-the-century craftsman home, Gramps' den was a shrine to his manly world of guns and hunting. It was totally different from the rest of the house, which reflected Granny's decorative sensibilities of lace curtains, wall-to-wall carpet, flowered wallpaper and stuffed chairs with embroidered doilies on their arms. As a kid, I was drawn to the den like a deer to cool water on a hot day. And it was okay for me to go in there. I think Gramps liked the idea of my spending hours alone in his den. My favorite time to be there was in the evening after dinner, as a summer sun dropped into the barely visible slice of the San Francisco Bay.

The Den was full of hunting, fishing, war, and sports memorabilia. On the hardwood floor sat a small oak table, draped with a tattered, balding deerskin. There were seven mounted deer heads peering variously around the room with their beady glass eyes, a few sets of deer and antelope antlers, a stuffed pheasant, and an open gun rack with seven rifles and shotguns. A locked Mission secretary Gramps had converted to a gun cabinet held three more rifles, and a holstered pistol-sized U.S. Navy flare gun was nailed to the wall.

Above the couch hung a three-foot long black and white panoramic photo of Gramps and his fellow U.S. Infantrymen of Company A, 310th Engineers, taken in July 1919 in Brest, France, just as these lucky survivors of the Great War were preparing finally to come home. The wallpaper depicted scenes of a noble Canadian Mountie: here, in a canoe exploring and conquering Nature; there, just having dismounted his horse, saluting with his right hand to a group of friendly Indians sitting in front of their teepee.

Through the window on the south side of the Den I'd cast my gaze through the giant redwood trees in the backyard, over the rooftops of Oakland's flatlands homes, and focus on a slice of the Bay Bridge. I'd hole up in that room, peer out through a two inch opening in the curtains, and fight off hordes of Krauts, imagining myself the hero on my favorite TV show, "Combat." I had a full arsenal and used it wisely. Starting with the

Gramps in his den (Circa 1960).

old lever-action Winchester rifle, I'd fire at the Bridge, knocking off Krauts at long-range as they headed into Oakland.

Pvt. LittleJohn gasped in desperation, "Sarge, they just keep coming! There are too many of them!"

I calmly soothed my junior charges with my signature Sergeant Saunders words of firm encouragement, and switched to my closer-range weapons. I blasted away, rapidly dry-firing the M-1 semi-automatic carbine, knowing that it had a fifteen-shot clip. Eventually, as they entered the yard and began to climb the walls of the house toward me, I'd pop a flare over the neighborhood, and then pull out the double-barreled 12-gauge shotgun to finish them off. They never had a chance.

When I grew bored with the carnage of war and the relentless cocking and dry-firing of weapons, I'd sit down at Gramps' four-post Mission oak desk, on which he'd placed a thick sheet of beveled glass to cover important photos: shots of grandchildren, including one of two-year-old me in a white mini-blazer and short pants, hair slicked back, standing next to a bow-tied Gramps, atop the hood of his 1952 Chevy Coupe Deluxe; a shot of my cousin Nancy in her lacy Easter finest; and one of my teenaged sister Terry with her pre-British Invasion hairsprayed beehive. All of these small photos surrounded the desktop's centerpiece: an 8X10 black-and-white of Dad in Cal's Memorial Stadium, in some long-past pre-War football Saturday, wearing his #56 and busting tackle at mid-field with what looked like a smile on his face, seeming to reflect the knowledge that this is A Moment In Life, the salience of which would never be approached again.

I'd yank the pull-chain of the brass desk lamp, illuminating the photographs under the glass, and I'd raid Gramps' stash: a full carton of Pep-O-Mint Lifesavers. Gramps always carried a roll in his pocket. At Sunday church, as the German Lutheran pastor hurled down the fire and brimstone and my sisters and I began to fidget, Gramps would quietly reach into his pocket, take out a roll of Pep-O-Mints, deliberately peel back the paper, and offer each of us a lifesaver. The minty sweetness of the lifesaver slowly melting in my mouth was thrillingly sinful.

I sucked on a lifesaver as I explored Gramps' desktop: an open pack of Old Gold cigarettes, a copper ashtray that Gramps had set into a deer antler, and a paperback, usually some Western novel lying jacket-up, open at the spine. Gramps also kept his silver cigarette lighter on his desk, along with a yellow and blue tin of lighter fluid. I'd squirt a little puddle of the fluid on the glass, light it, and thrill at the flame hovering over, but not burning, my cousin's white Easter dress, Terry's ratted 'do, and a thousand Cal undergrads

This 8X10 of Dad running for Cal was the centerpiece atop Gramps' desk.

cheering Dad's blast up the middle. The flame flared dramatically but quickly died back to a cool flickering blue, before popping out—gone like those past football Saturdays, leaving no trace of its momentary glory.

In the den, when I was still young, the mysteries of Gramps' life soaked right into my pores. Its simplicity, rather than revealing a transparent truth about the man, cracked open doors to secret tales—sad and perhaps violent stories of war, and of hunting trips decades earlier. All mostly behind him now, like that faded and dusty deerskin with the pattern baldness.

One evening, when I was about ten, Gramps came in on me as I was playing with his guns. He looked at me approvingly and smiled: "Come here, my boy, I'll show you something."

He produced a small skeleton key, unlocked the drawers and drop leaf of his gun cabinet, sat me down next to him at his desk and began to share what to me were unbelievable treasures: pre-revolution Russian coins and currency, knives and guns, old hunting and fishing licenses. As he revealed these mementos, he'd tell me little stories about them.

Once, in a near whisper, Gramps said, "The gun cabinet, and everything inside it, goes to you after I'm gone." Frustrated, I suppose, with my dumb silence, he blurted out, his voice breaking with emotion that startled me, "This is your *heritage*!"

That night, and on subsequent nights afterwards, these artifacts served as an entrée for him to tell me about his life.

Gramps was born April 30, 1896, in Hubbell, one of a cluster of small working class towns on the frigid upper peninsula of Northern Michigan, dominated by the copper mines and mills of Calumet and Hecla Mining Company. Russell took his mother's last name. It was written right there on his birth certificate—"Illegitimate"—and even 70 or 80 years later, as an aging grandfather, he was still shamed to silence over the fact that he had no father. In 1895, eighteen-year-old Annie Messner had met Thomas Cashell, the son of a well-off German family who was visiting the Hubbell area. They courted and she became pregnant. Scandalized, Cashell's family shipped him home. Annie gave birth to the baby but she could not raise him. Instead, her brother John Messner and his wife Dora took Russell in.

If somebody asked Gramps why his uncle raised him, he replied with a tersely humorous story: "One day I was sitting on the fence in front of my mom's home when my uncle walked by and asked me, 'Want to come over for dinner?' 'What're you havin'?' 'Beans.' 'I *love* beans,' I said, and I went home with him for dinner, and stayed."

Other stories of his youth and family were similarly terse, and coded as though they were tall tales that stood for some deeper truth. Once, sitting at his desk, he slipped off the reddish gold ring that he always wore on his left pinky finger, and set it with an audible click on the glass.

"This is made of Black Hills gold and Lake Superior agate," he said, "and it'll be yours when I'm gone. I inherited it from my uncle, and before that, it belonged to my uncle's friend, J.P. Kelly," and he showed me the name "J.P. Kelly," engraved inside the ring.

Then he pulled an old nickel-plated snub-nosed .32 revolver out of the gun cabinet, and set it down, next to the ring.

"The pistol and the ring go together," he said with a reverence I could not understand. "J.P. Kelly owned a mine, and after he lost it in a poker game, he blew his brains out with this gun. My uncle ended up with the ring and the gun; he left them for me, said that they were to stay together. When I'm gone, my boy, they belong to you. And they go together."

Gramps' edict was clear, but I was intrigued with the deeper mysteries of the ring and the gun. For decades, I puzzled over the significance of this dubious inheritance.

Gramps grew up with hunting and fishing as a way of life that helped to supplement the family's food supply. After finishing the eighth grade, he went to work in the copper mill in the nearby town of Lake Linden, where Granny was raised. In the first decade of the twentieth century, the copper industry was booming, but the workers—including those like Gramps, a teenager working at the mill—were "paid nothing." When the Western Federation of Miners demanded an eight-hour workday, a three-dollar a day minimum wage, the elimination of the dangerous one-man drill, and the right to represent the mine and mill workers, the company refused. Gramps joined those who waged what turned out to be a bloody year-long strike from 1913-1914. Calumet & Hecla out-waited the strikers and broke the union efforts. The experience made Gramps a lifelong union man, distrustful of "fat cats," and "crooks" who didn't work with their hands, whether of the industrial, political, or academic stripe. One of my earliest memories of Gramps is a cold, foggy morning, when our family drove him across the Bay Bridge to San Francisco and dropped him off at Schmidt Lithograph, to walk a picket line.

After the copper strike ended in April 1914, Gramps' work in the smelter shifted to the refining process that removed silver from the copper ore. It was hot work, and one of his jobs, he told me with a mischievous glint, was to test the molten silver to be sure it was hot enough.

"I dipped out a little scoop of the metal, and watched it harden. It formed a little disc about the size of a two-bit piece"—he made a little circle with his thumb and forefinger to show me—"You were supposed to throw it back in the smelter, but sometimes I'd keep it, and that wasn't easy. When you come to work, you had to take off all your clothes, and then go in to another room and put on your work clothes. Same when you left work. So they could watch you. Make sure you weren't helping yourself to some of the goods, you see? But I figured out how. They let you bring your lunch pail in, and I hollowed out space in the handle. I'd put that silver two-bit piece in there and walk out with it. Not every day. Just sometimes."

One piece of silver, he told me, doubled his weekly wage.

To my ten-year old ears, this was the most deliciously transgressive story I'd ever heard. I was stunned by Gramps' easy sense that stealing was okay; it ran against everything I'd been taught, that stealing is *always wrong*. But I came to realize that Gramps' feelings of right and wrong were forged in his teens, in the heat of labor's effort to unionize the mills. The lesson he learned was that the scales were unfairly tipped toward the rich owners. Helping himself to a little on the side seemed not only fair, but *just*. And taking just a little, not being greedy, fit with his German Lutheran ethic of hard work and a modest lifestyle. "Everything in moderation," Gramps would say as he gave me a sip of his wine at the dinner table, under the silent and seemingly disapproving eye of my father.

There was a difference between having a drink every night and being a drunk. And there was a difference between taking a two-bit-sized piece of silver from your employer and extorting millions of dollars in profits from your workers.

Gramps' life in the copper mills ended after the United States declared war against Germany on April 6, 1917. A year later, at the age of 22, Gramps was sent to Russia with the U.S. Army's Expeditionary Forces. "I guess they figured us boys from the Upper Peninsula could handle the cold," he explained to me with a laugh.

Sixty years later, when I was living with Gramps as a grad student, I did some reading about the Great War and wanted to get him talking about it. I cooked us a good dinner, one of his favorite recipes that Granny used to make: country spareribs buried in sauerkraut and red potatoes, slow-baked in a casserole, and served with cold applesauce. As we ate, I told him that I'd read a book by a historian, who said that when the U.S. entered the Great War, young men were so excited they couldn't wait to go. Modernity had undermined men's traditional ways of proving themselves, and a good manly war seemed just the ticket for shoring up their sagging masculinity. Gramps listened quietly as he leaned into his pork and kraut, his face mostly hidden behind the ubiquitous red visor. My story done, he peeked up from under his visor and made brief eye contact with me, glanced down momentarily at his fork as though carefully choosing his words, looked up again and barked at me, mouth still full of food, *"I was drafted!"*

Face reburied in his plate, he muttered disparagingly, *"*Masculinity!— kinda' *crap* they teaching you up at that university!?"

4
Guns

I'd nearly shot Gramps. The three of us had been walking a quail hunt, Dad a bit behind me on the left, Gramps a few steps ahead on my right. The double-barreled 4-10 shotgun Dad had given me last year for my eleventh birthday was cradled in my left arm, safely pointed down. With sudden thunder a covey of quail erupted to our right. I flicked off the safety with my thumb and remembered Dad's lesson: never shoot at the whole covey; instead, pick one bird, swing your gun in an arc, lead the target, squeeze and fire. I did this with perfection, dropping the bird.

My moment of triumph was stillborn. I knew exactly what I had done wrong: the swing of my gun barrel had passed directly across Gramps' body. During the shot, I'd had a gestalt-like awareness of everything—my body, the gun, Gramps, the bird—and I was certain, then and still today, that there was no way I'd come close to pulling the trigger while Gramps was in my line of fire. But still, I'd lost face, and perhaps Dad's and Gramps' trust. I'd broken the first rule of gun safety: Never point a gun at anybody. Gramps hadn't budged since the shot; he stood squinting at me, his twelve-gauge resting on his shoulder. I was frozen in place. Dad walked up and asked, "Do you see what you did? Did you see Gramps there?"

I stared at the ground, "Yes." I looked up, "I'm sorry, Gramps."

"Okay," he said noncommittally. Then he glanced toward the dead bird and offered me the finest possible absolution: "That was a hell of a wing shot."

> 12/25/34
>
> To My Son:
>
> This Present to you my Son Represents the fullfillment of one of my dreams. I have always looked forward to the time when we could both go out to-gether in the mutual companionship of a good dog and a pair of guns which we both could appreciate and use inteligently.
>
> Remember Two things:
> Never point it at anybody
> Always make sure it is unloaded when not in use.
>
> "May you enjoy it as much as your Dad always has"
>
> Your Pal & Dad
>
> Dec. 25th 1934

Gramps' 1934 Christmas letter to his son.

The year he was fourteen, Dad received a special gift from Gramps for Christmas. On the envelope, Gramps wrote:

To My Son
Christmas Day
Dec. 25, 1934

Inside was a three-page letter, written in pencil in Gramps' finest hand.

To My Son:

This Present to you my Son Represents the fullfillment of one of my dreams. I have always looked forward to the time when we could both go out to-gether in the mutual companionship of a good dog and a pair of guns which we both could appreciate and use inteligently. Therefore these few words of advise. A good gun in the hands of a fool is as great a menace to the general Public as a contagious disease. In the hands of a person with common sense, It is a pleasure & source of healthful exercise if indulged with common sense. It can be an instrument of terrible destruction if not used right. Always keep it pointed away from you and your companion, with whom you are out.

Remember only <u>one shot</u> may cause you a life's Regret if it goes off when pointed in the wrong direction. If you do not harm yourself it may be some one dear to you. Never load your gun and carry in a car. Always make sure it is unloaded before you put it away. 7 out of 10 accidents always end with this answer "I did not know it was loaded," and gunpowder and liquor never mix, I do not have to caution you at your age about that part but you will propably go out with <u>other people</u> as you go older & you will have to caution them to protect your own life and & interests.

You know my son a machine will Run just as good as the care it gets. So always keep your guns clean & well oiled. If you abuse your body you must pay for it, the same applies to your guns. A gun is a piece of machinery the same as your body. Any more question you may care to ask I will always be glad to answer. Always remember two things:

<u>*Never point it at anybody*</u>
<u>*Always make sure it is unloaded when not in use.*</u>

"May you enjoy it as much as you Dad always has"
Your <u>Pal</u> & <u>Dad</u>
RJM
Dec. 25th
1934

Dad kept that letter in his top drawer, with his socks. When Mom gave me the letter after Dad died, I felt as though I'd read it before. Dad had delivered these same words of caution to me, almost verbatim, the first time he handed me a .22 rifle to shoot at a tin can. And he continued to reiterate the rules of gun safety and hunting etiquette every time we went hunting. Hunting is fun, but guns are deadly and must be treated with sober intelligence, respect, and awe. This message was hammered home and punctuated with vague references to Dad and Gramps having witnessed in war the terrible things that guns were capable of. This grim reverence for the horrific potential of guns sat uneasily alongside the heroic fantasies burgeoning in my imagination.

By the time I was three, I was fully indoctrinated into a fantasy world of guns, hunting, and war. In 1955, I was caught up in a national "Crockett Craze." Disney's popular movie about the rugged individualist, Indian-fighter, and martyr of the Alamo Davy Crockett was followed by a TV series. Suddenly, boys throughout America were riding one of the first television-driven consumer waves. I worshipped the lanky actor Fess Parker, and owned a 33-RPM record of the Davy Crockett songs that I memorized. Like seemingly every little boy in America, and some girls too, I sported a coonskin cap.

Intrigued especially with the legend that Crockett was "raised in the woods where he knew every tree; killed him a b'ar when he was only three," I took the coonskin cap fad several steps further and made my own fashion statement. From the tanned hide of a buck that Dad had killed, Mom designed and sewed me a genuine buckskin coat and pants, abundantly fringed and adorned with colorful Davy Crockett stencils. I accessorized with a plastic tomahawk sheathed to my waist, a "Davy Crockett Original Powderhorn" slung across my shoulder, and a flintlock pistol with a real metal hammer you could cock and fire, just like Davy at the Alamo. "Here comes Davy Crewcut," Dad laughed as I strutted into the room in full gear. I was King of the Wild Frontier—or at least of the spanking new suburban landscape I labored to protect from the wild Indians I was certain were still holed up in the nearby mountains of the Salinas Valley.

My Davy Crockett persona was the opening chapter of a childhood of heroic gun fantasy. It was a way for me to anticipate becoming a hunter, like Dad and Gramps. I'd repeatedly aim and fire my plastic pistol at Joe, the handsome three-point buck Dad had mounted directly above my bed. (Mom's Aunt Bobbie endeared herself to me forever when, visiting from

Russell Sr. and Russell Jr. "in the mutual companionship of a good dog and a pair of guns" (Circa 1930).

Michael A. Messner

King of the Wild Suburb (1955).

Illinois, she entered my bedroom, glanced up at Joe's head and said, "Neato, Mike. Now let's walk around the wall to see the rest of him.")

My attire progressed from Davy Crockett coonskin to John Wayne cowboy hat, and by the early 1960's I became a Mercury astronaut. After dinner every night, unbeknownst to my family, I'd blast off right out of town. As Linny and Terry did the dishes, I'd steal away to the tiny half-bathroom just off the kitchen. I'd open the drawer of the built-in dresser, bumping it against the door handle, so no one could enter. Pants at my ankles, seated on the john, I'd press in secret sequence three tiny buttons—holes I'd dug into the wood with a pencil—and my rocket would begin to vibrate. After a short countdown I'd have liftoff, my latrine-turned-Mercury Atlas Rocket rising right out of the house at 801 Bautista Drive, singeing the roof of Donnie Hallstone's home, arcing over the lettuce fields of the Salinas Valley, and blasting into orbit, just like John Glenn.

One autumn evening, on my return from outer space, I exited the bathroom to find the kitchen empty and the front door wide open. Puzzled, I stepped out the front door and found Linny walking toward me from next door, crying.

"Ray killed himself," she said.

Ray Bennett lived next door with his thin, sharp-tongued wife Marion. He called me Mikeyo, and Hardrock, and dispensed advice to kids, as in "Mikeyo, have fun; but have *clean* fun." Ray drove around in a company car, doing something or other for Richfield Oil. One day, for some reason, I drove around with him, and he stopped at a bar on Alisal Street, as I sat fidgeting in the car. I'd heard my parents whisper that Ray drank. I knew that this meant he drank during the day. One late night, I was awakened when I heard him rapping on his bedroom window, slurring "Marion? Marion, c'mon now. Let me in, Marion."

When I asked Mom why Marion and Ray didn't have kids—I knew every married couple was supposed to have kids—she replied sadly, "I don't know, honey. Maybe they just don't love each other enough."

But they did love Linny. Marion and Ray kind of adopted her—she had dinners at their house, took vacations with them to The Salton Sea, Disneyland, and a family ranch they called Bee-Rock.

This evening, when Marion arrived home from her job at the Credit Bureau, she opened the garage door and found Ray with the back of his head blown off from a shotgun blast to the mouth. Earlier that day, Dad had come home from the high school for lunch, and Ray had phoned and asked to borrow the shotgun he'd sold Dad a year earlier. Dad had handed it to Ray over the back fence. Now I could hear Marion next door, imploring Dad, "But *why*, Russ? Why did you *give* it to him?"

Poor Dad moaned, "He said he was going rabbit hunting."

That night, in what seemed a kind of penance, Dad cleaned Ray's blood and brains from Marion's garage. I was dazed with the realization that there wasn't some specialist—someone from the police, the mortuary, the U.S. Government or Richfield Oil—whose job it was to clean up after somebody who'd made a mess of things with his own suicide. A year later, when I saw the photos of Jackie Kennedy, her stylish suit splattered with her husband's blood, it occurred to me that some guy—someone like Dad who understood the dirty work of war—probably had to clean the President's blood and brains from the inside of that shiny convertible in Dallas.

Ray Bennett's death brought home to me something I already knew: guns can have ugly, tragically devastating effects. Several years later, I decided I didn't want to live with guns, and now today as a father I don't want to pass to my sons any sort of pro-gun legacy. But I also have little patience for what passes as "the guns debate" in this country. Those knee-jerk gun control advocates who vilify hunters as pinheaded drunks careening around the wild in their off-road vehicles, tossing empty beer cans and shooting at anything that moves should read Gramps' letter to his fourteen-year-old son. Or they should peruse one of Jimmy Carter's beautifully spiritual essays about hunting, fishing and the outdoors. Hunters like President Carter share a deep reverence for the animals they kill and eat; they are committed to the preservation of the natural environment, and they have an uncompromising adherence to the rules of gun safety. There are about 12,000 firearms deaths in the U.S. annually. On average, only one of these deaths per year results from accidental shootings by hunters.

Animal rights advocates, it seems to me, operate from a deeply-felt and morally consistent set of beliefs. However, much anti-hunting sentiment is ignorant middle-class snobbery, expressed in morally inconsistent ways by the very same people who think nothing about slicing into their ranch-tortured filet mignon. On the other hand, hunters have done little to allay the negative stereotypes that people hold of them. Instead, hunters have too often been sucked into extremist right wing paranoia about protecting second amendment rights, thus defending the indefensible: ownership of assault rifles and concealable handguns. When I hear gun owners claiming a constitutional right to own weapons designed only to kill other people, perhaps so that they can fight off the Black Helicopters secretly deployed by their own government, I can't help but imagine Dad and Gramps shaking their heads in dismay. Hunters, I believe, should be in the forefront of pushing for strictly enforced and sane gun control. Most gun deaths do not result from hunting rifles or shotguns. And you don't need an assault rifle to hunt quail.

○

When Gramps died in 1981, the extended family descended on the old home to collect keepsakes, and I announced that I didn't want any of the rifles or shotguns, though I knew some—like the old Winchester—were collectors' items. I just didn't want to live with guns in my home. I still don't. Well, that's not entirely true. I do own one gun. Locked in the drawer of Gramps' gun cabinet in my study is the .32 revolver that was the last thing J.P. Kelly ever held in his hand. Gramps told me that the gun had to stay with the ring, and I have honored his wish by keeping both.

When he was deeply troubled, Ethan Allen Hawley, the middle-aged protagonist of John Steinbeck's *The Winter of Our Discontent*, cradles in his hands a blown-glass paperweight, a family talisman passed down through the generations of Hawley men. While Hawley's talisman transmits comforting warmth into him in times of discontent, J.P. Kelly's pistol sits coldly in my locked drawer, representing simultaneously the unimaginable lights-out moment of a bullet to the brain, and a warm moment of connection, where Gramps passed something important and meaningful, on to me.

For most of my life, I've wondered: what is this pistol supposed to mean to me? What is the right thing do with it? Am I obliged to pass it on, with the ring, to my sons? If I do pass the gun on to Miles and Sasha, how does that square with my hopes to break the intergenerational cycle of violence that gets passed on from fathers to their sons, and to their sons? I once considered simply getting rid of this gun. Maybe, I thought, I'll sell it to a gun collector; however, that would only mean that it could end up in the hands of some other boy. More than once, I fantasized pitching the gun off of a bridge into a deep river as a small but dramatic gesture of my hope to purge the world of violence, starting with my own family talisman. But if I got rid of the gun, I knew I would be failing to honor Gramps' solemn edict to keep the gun and the ring together, and pass them on as twin family talismans to future Messners.

On July 1, 2008—my fifty-sixth birthday—I sat in a circle with Miles, Sasha and my wife Pierrette in our back yard, in the shade of rustling palm

Michael A. Messner

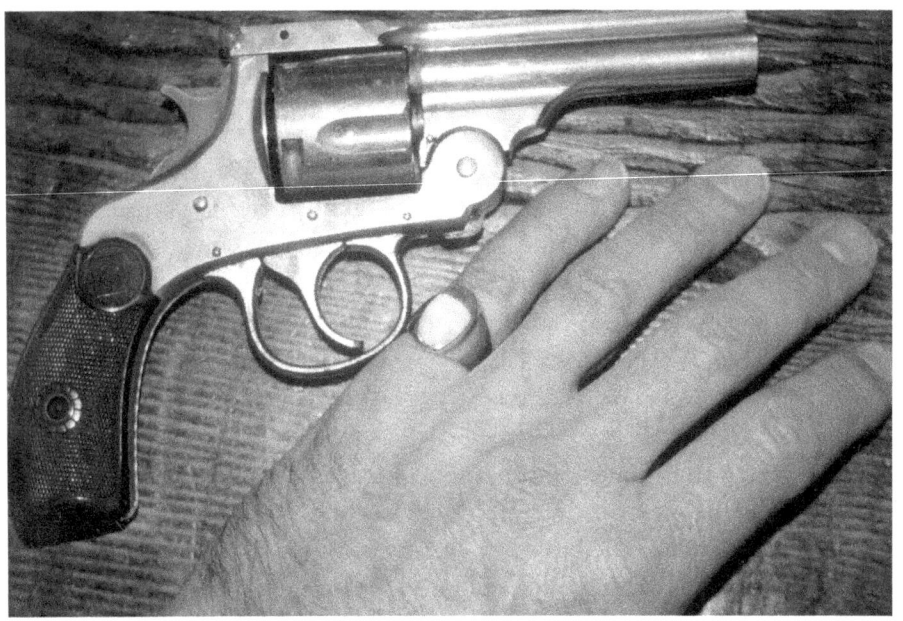

Gramps asked me to keep J. P. Kelly's ring and pistol.

trees and bamboo. I passed around the ring, and then the revolver, to each of my family members. They each slipped the ring on a finger, before passing it on, and gingerly inspected the pistol as I reiterated the family story of J.P. Kelly, and of Gramps telling me that the ring and the gun have to stay together. I told them—not for the first time—that this had presented me with a dilemma.

We then moved into our cabaña, where I had set up a vise on a table. I placed the pistol tightly in the vise—taking care to couch it in leather, so as not to scar the metal—and pulled back the hammer, revealing the gun's firing pin. I then picked up a hacksaw, and made the first cut into the quarter-inch thick steel base of the firing pin. I handed the saw to Pierrette, who took a few strokes, and she then passed the saw to Miles, who extended the cut with strong, rapid strokes. Sasha finished the job, the severed firing pin skipping harmlessly across the cement floor.

With Gramps' ring on my finger, and the now-defanged pistol in my hand, I declared that I would continue to keep these two family talismans together, so that the legacy of intergenerational love intended by Gramps could be passed on to my two sons, albeit in altered form. A ring is often said to symbolize love, an eternal circle of life. A gun symbolizes death. The violent past of the Messner .32 revolver lives on in the cold steely story of J.P. Kelly's suicide. But this pistol can never again fire a bullet; the fresh ragged scar on the pistol's hammer testifies that the gun's violent potential is now purged, fully and finally.

But I realize too that I can no more fix the meaning of the ring and the gun for my sons' future than I can definitively discern what these two objects truly meant to Gramps, much less to his Uncle John or J.P. Kelly before him. I have, for the moment, created my own meaning for the ring and the gun. The pistol sits once again in the dark locked drawer of Gramps' gun cabinet, awaiting Miles and Sasha, and perhaps future generations of Messners, who will handle it, wonder at its past, and conjure their own meanings.

5
A Boy and His Dog

"I'm afraid I have some bad news, Pal. Tiger died today."

Dad's words made no sense at all. I had just walked in the back door of the garage, my jeans caked with muddy grass stains, a football tucked under my arm. Dad had heard me coming and stepped into the garage to tell me the news in private. I knew that earlier that day, Dad, Gramps and Terry had driven to Chualar Canyon with Tiger, just to take a little hike. What could have happened? Tiger was barely two years old—still a pup. Just that morning, I'd wrestled with him on the living room floor.

"How?—what?"

"The ranchers put out some coyote bait—strychnine, I guess—and Tiger got into it. He just started convulsing and died in Gramps' arms. There was nothing we could do."

I burst into tears.

"I know," Dad said. "I got a little teary-eyed myself."

Dad's words affirmed that he expected I'd be upset. But it also was a signal that I should have my cry here in the garage and enter the house dry-eyed. I guessed that was why he'd come out to the garage to tell me the news, so I'd not have to hear it in front of the whole family. I was nine, and had already internalized the rule that real men—strong men like Dad—keep their emotions to themselves. I took a couple of heaving breaths, and Dad put his hand on my shoulder.

"Okay to go in now?"

"Yeah, I guess so."

We stepped through the door. Gramps, Granny and Terry sat somberly at the kitchen table, and Mom stood at the stove. I felt their eyes on me. They all knew how close I had been to this dog. Many times, as I'd wrestled on the carpet with Tiger or lain intertwined with him as I watched TV, Granny or Gramps would smile at me and say wistfully, "A boy and his dog." In their gaze, we were more than just "Mike and Tiger." The two of us symbolized for them an iconic Norman Rockwell Americana snapshot.

I felt this too, my larger-than-life bond with Tiger. I'd taught him to sit and stay. When I said "Gimme five," he'd raise his paw and shake hands with me. I'd break chunks of dog biscuit and zip them one at a time directly at the spot between Tiger's eyes, and he'd catch every one, just like Jimmy Davenport, the Giants' Golden Gloved third baseman spearing line drives. I'd trained Tiger to come to me when I'd blow my supersonic dog whistle that people couldn't hear. He was the family dog, yes, but I saw the two of us through Granny and Gramps' eyes. I imagined Tiger to be mine.

Gramps was first to speak, and there were tears in his eyes. "He died quickly, my boy. I tried to hold him down, but it was no good."

Gramps showed me his hand, a bloody gash of skin torn away just above his thumb. I knew that sweet Tiger would never bite anybody. Seeming to read my mind, Gramps said, "He didn't know what he was doing. It was the poison."

A tear spilled over on to Gramps' cheek, and he dabbed it away. My lesson from Dad was that it's okay to get "a little teary-eyed"—but a real man controls himself and doesn't let the tears spill over. It shows strength to control yourself in this way. I'd seen Gramps cry many times—unapologetically shedding sentimental tears while telling a family story, and now, while talking about Tiger's death. As a little kid, it embarrassed me to see Gramps weep; he was clearly not as strong as Dad, I knew. Years later as a young man, as I began to broaden my own sense of manhood, I came to admire the ease with which Gramps revealed his tender feelings.

Tiger's was the first loss through death that I ever experienced. Today, you hear stories every day of kids seeing terrible acts of violence and death—in wars, on the streets, in their own homes. Even in my day, some kids had to endure the early death of a parent or a sibling. When my friend Jon Scattini's little sister Mary Anne died suddenly in the early 1960's, I felt second-hand the reverberations of unfathomable family grief. But I did not experience a death in my immediate family until 1977 when Dad died. During my sheltered and idyllic childhood, death was almost entirely an abstraction.

For many people lucky not to have to endure the death of a loved one during our childhoods, pets taught us about loss and grief. It sure was so for me. When I was six years old, our family lost twelve-year old Lady, the Springer Spaniel named after the star of the Disney movie "Lady and the Tramp." Mom and Dad purchased Lady in 1947, the same year Terry was born. Lady became the first of a long string of dogs that Terry would love in her abbreviated lifetime. Our Lady was a runner, frequently escaping the house for a few hours before returning. But on a family visit to Oakland, she got out of Gramps' yard and never came back. We advertised in the newspaper and posted "lost dog" notices on telephone poles, all to no avail.

On the third day after Lady's disappearance, Mom told me in the gentlest way possible that it was time to give up hope: "Just imagine that a nice family has found Lady and is taking good care of her."

Instead, I imagined that Lady had been crushed by one of those huge busses that roared up and down busy Claremont Avenue, or that she was wandering lost, hungry and old with no familiar bearings in this strange huge city. I retreated upstairs and plopped down on the floor next to my bed, weeping loudly. Dad came in and told me that it was time to stop crying now, that my tears wouldn't bring Lady back.

"We'll get another dog," Dad promised.

A few months after Lady's departure, we got Tiger, a six-week-old bundle of orange and white with razor-sharp puppy teeth. We bought him just outside Salinas from a breeder named Herman Johnson, a tall, rail-thin fiftyish guy in overalls who always looked like he hadn't shaved for a couple of days. I had never met an Okie, but I imagined that kindly Herman Johnson was one. He moved with slow lanky strides and spoke in a quiet drawl that didn't sound Californian. Herman specialized in breeding Brittany Spaniels, medium-sized dogs with distinctive orange mottling and freckles on white.

As we followed Herman Johnson's deliberate trudge up the hill from his house to the gleaming white kennels above, he said, "This here Brittany Spaniel is a great bird dog. Your dad'll love him with the quail, Mike." And, now glancing at Mom, "And he's good with kids, Ma'am—a fine family dog."

Herman was right. I immediately loved Tiger. There was no question in my mind that love was what you would call my feeling for this dog. I'd play-fight with Tiger, and he'd growl and bite me ever-so-softly, pulling his punches like a thoughtful sparring partner. Gramps said approvingly that Tiger had the "soft mouth" that you'd want in a good bird dog. In our backyard lived two Frisbee-sized turtles named Pokey and Speedy that we'd taken from a river. Tiger would frequently pick up a turtle in his mouth and walk around the yard with it, the leather reptile's legs slowly paddling the air as it tried to free itself. But Tiger never seemed to injure the turtles; we joked that Pokey and Speedy were Tiger's pets. He was a gentle dog, and I knew that he'd never hurt me. When I'd curl up with him on the floor, underneath a table, stroking the soft puppy-pink skin of his belly, I knew that Tiger loved me too.

Dad declared that he *liked* dogs, but that he could never *love* a dog, not after what he'd seen in war. A human being, Dad said, is irreplaceable; as much as you might like a dog, it's just an animal, easily replaced. Gramps could be very sentimental about his dogs. But once, when I declared that I loved Tiger, he shook his finger at me and insisted that it was not possible to love a dog. Gramps presented this as a general law of the universe: "You can't love an inanimate object," he'd say.

I knew, even as an eight-year old, that Gramps was misusing the word "inanimate" to describe a dog, but I took his meaning to be that people can only truly love human beings, not animals. I wasn't about to disagree openly with Gramps. But I knew what I felt.

All of the adults around me seemed equivocal about their feelings for dogs. Granny often said, "I like dogs, but I like them in their place," which meant outdoors.

Mom too liked dogs, though she complained about "all that dog hair" that was constantly appearing on the kitchen floor, the carpet, and her clothing.

I loved Tiger, even more than I'd loved Lady before him. And I think my feeling for those dogs was grounded in the way that Mom made them seem to be real members of the family. She engaged in comical personification with our family dogs, ventriloquizing for each of them with a distinctive high, whiny voice. When I rolled around on the floor with Tiger, hugged him and kissed his velvety cheek, he'd say "I love you, kid. How about a kiss on the lips?" He always called me "kid." As I munched a salami sandwich in the backyard, Tiger sat attentively staring at me, and begged, "C'mon, kid. Just a little bite, *please?*" Often, Tiger was a real wise-ass. If I'd toss him the heel of my bread but no salami, he'd catch it, spit it out on the ground, look up at me and exclaim, "Oh goddamn! Chintzy kid!"

When Tiger died, I was crushed. But Mom and Dad promised that we'd get another dog soon. I had learned after Lady how quickly you can shift your affection to a new dog. Herman Johnson had a Brittany Spaniel bitch who was going to drop a litter in a few weeks. One of those pups, he said, would be Mike's dog.

○

I heard the click, followed by the low electronic hummmm of Mom and Dad's clock radio coming to life. I popped out of my bed, my bare feet quickly scurrying across the cool floor, into my parent's bedroom. Dad had already scrunched to the center of the bed, closer to Mom, and pulled the covers open so I could climb in next to him, as I did on every weekday morning. As I settled in to the warmth of my parents' bed, Dad stretched his right arm across my pillow, and I rested my head on his forearm. Dad's forearm, shaped like Popeye's, was anything but pillow-like; I imagined this was more like resting my head on a steel girder, or on Superman's arm. But there was comfort in that discomfort.

Mom and Dad's clock radio alarm was timed so that they could doze a few minutes before getting up, while listening to Paul Harvey's morning news and commentary. Paul Harvey's conservatism appealed to Dad. Once, while reporting a story about a union that was trying to get profit-sharing benefits for its workers, Harvey quipped sarcastically, "Well, I guess that would be understandable if the workers were willing also to share the risk." Dad, lying on his back with eyes closed, muttered, "That's right." I liked Paul Harvey's homey anecdotes, and his upbeat marking of the seasons. It sent a thrill through me when, one morning as fall turned to winter, Paul Harvey proclaimed the end of football season and cheerily told us that "It's time to put on those basketball shorts."

When Paul Harvey closed his daily report with his signature, "Paul Harvey...*Good day!*"—he always held a pregnant pause before uttering his sharply upbeat "*Good day!*"—we knew it was time for us to get up. I'd scamper to my room and start to get dressed. Mom would start rattling around in the kitchen, preparing five breakfasts and sack lunches for three kids. Dad headed for the bathroom to shave and take a quick shower—he always took "quick showers"—there was no lingering, squandered motion or wasted water. As he shaved in front of the mirror, I could hear him warming up his morning voice, saying to himself, "Paul Harvey...*Good Day!*" Or he'd sing an ad jingle we'd just heard on the radio: "No salt salts like Morton Salt salts."

Mom, who had perfect pitch, would laugh and yell into the bathroom telling Dad that he had it wrong, that he needed to raise his voice a half-octave on the second "salts," and she'd show him, overemphasizing it: "No salt *salts* like Morton Salt salts."

Mom sang it like the real deal; I could just imagine her pretty voice performing this jingle on the radio. When Dad sang the Morton Salt song, it sounded like the soundtrack to the Bataan Death March.

One morning, as the three of us lay listening to Paul Harvey, the phone rang. Mom answered it and handed it to me, the cord stretching across Dad's prone body. I sat up in bed, wondering who in the world would be calling me so early in the morning.

"Hello there, Mike?" Man's voice; Okie drawl. "This is Herman Johnson callin' to tell ya that last night yer dog was born, Mike."

"Oh!—When—?"

"Well, it'll be five, maybe six weeks bufir ya kin take 'im home, Mike. But ya kin come out here with yer Mom bufir that, and pick out yer dog, okay?"

"Okay—*Okay!*"

Without saying any more, I reached across Dad and Mom and slammed the phone into its cradle. "That was Herman Johnson! My dog was born and we can go pick him out soon. I'm gonna call him Tiger."

"Whoa," said Mom. "Didn't you even thank Mr. Johnson?"

Mom called Herman right back and thanked him. A couple of weeks later, we went out to pick out the dog that would become Tiger II. Four weeks after that, he joined our family. I proceeded immediately to plug Tiger II into the same slots of my life that the first Tiger had occupied. But he didn't fit. When I play-fought with him, his snarl was a real growl; his bite chomped a bit too hard. Inspecting the cuts and scrapes on my hands and arms, Dad surmised that maybe this Tiger just didn't have the soft mouth that the first Tiger had. But it turned out to be more than that. This dog preferred to cower underneath tables or in the backyard under the chaise longue, and if I'd try to climb under with him, he'd snarl at me. He seemed indifferent to my supersonic dog whistle. And any food play—including trying to train him to catch dog biscuits—proved dangerous; he got really aggressive around food. We talked about how he was "different," but we held for several months to the idea that Tiger was part of our family, that he'd "grow out of it" and calm down. But he didn't.

Then Tiger went after Donnie Hallstone. Donnie loved dogs. For years, Donnie hadn't been allowed to get his own dog, so we kind of shared our dogs with him. Skinny eight-year old Donnie Hallstone, all glasses and ears below his ever-present Rotary Little League baseball cap crouched down and extended his hand beneath the chaise longue to pet Tiger. The dog—our Bad Seed—snarled and snapped at Donnie's hand. That was it for Tiger, as far as my parents were concerned. No way was our dog going to threaten little Donnie Hallstone or any of the kids in the neighborhood.

We gave up on Tiger II and rejected him. I resisted this decision, at first; I knew this was not something you'd do with a family member, give up on him, send him away, trade him in for a replacement. But we did that with Tiger II. Like a once-promising rookie who, it turned out, couldn't hit the curve ball, he was sent back to the minors. Herman Johnson sent up a replacement puppy, a Brittany Spaniel female we named Jina. She turned out to be a good dog whose life spanned the twelve years from my late-childhood to my parents' transition to empty-nesters. I never got as close with Jina as I had been with Tiger. I took her on walks and played with her, but I was transitioning, too. I was less into envisioning myself posing in a "boy and his dog" Norman Rockwell painting and was increasingly interested in spending as much time as I could with my friends—away from home, family and dog. Within a few years, I was off to college. Jina got fat on junk food, including a daily sugar cube mom would pop to her as she'd pour her own morning coffee.

○

For Dad and Gramps, hunting—especially deer hunting—was an annual rite of father-and-son togetherness. More than anything else, hunting made them pals for life. A good hunting dog was a fundamental part of the package. This was codified in the opening two sentences of Gramps' 1934 Christmas letter to Dad that accompanied his gift of a hunting rifle: *"I have always looked forward to the time when we could both go out to-gether in the mutual companionship of a good dog and a pair of guns which we both could appreciate and use inteligently."* A decade after Gramps wrote that, Dad was overseas at war, sending his own letters back to Gramps, letters full of longing to be home so that they could go hunting. In June of 1944 from somewhere in the South Pacific, Dad wrote a warm Father's Day letter to Gramps, concluding with a greeting to their bird dog: *"Say hello to Pepper for me Dad!"* In his letters to his son, Gramps sent detailed descriptions of his hunting trips, and told of his plans to purchase a pointer. In February of 1945, now stationed in Chicago, Dad wrote back enthusiastically.

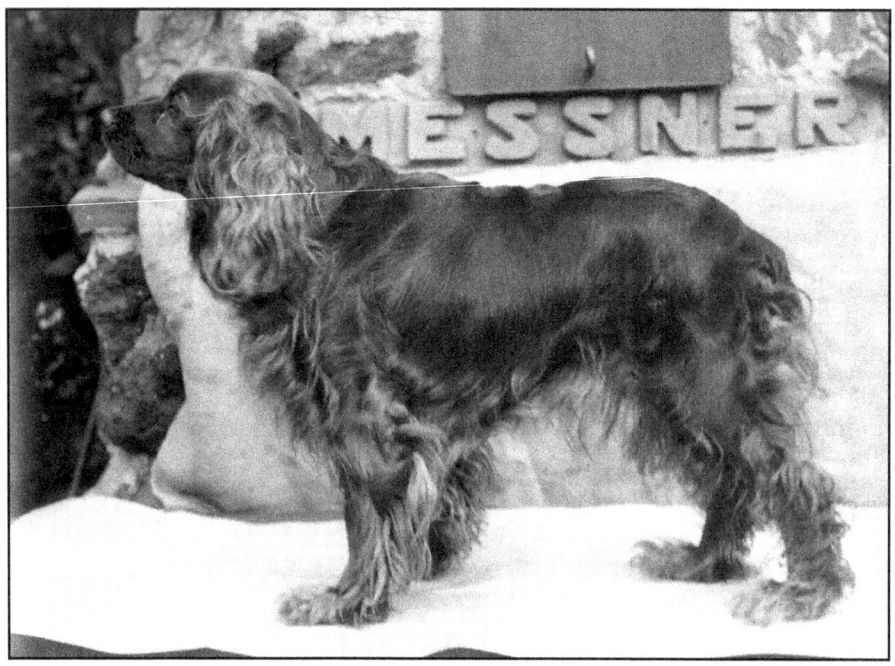

Stupido Tiger, on Gramps' backyard fireplace (Circa 1950).

Well old timer let me begin by thanking you for your swell letter…Sure was glad to hear that you are considering getting a pointer Dad. I'll bet Mom isn't too thrilled tho is she? Boy when this mess is over I'm sure going to get me a good deer hound.

A month later, Dad continued the excited exchange over dogs and hunting.

Sorry to hear the deal on the Pointer fell thru Dad. Sure would like to try one of those dogs. If this war ever gets over we are really going to go in for this business in a big way. I'm going to get a real good deer Hound.

After the war, Gramps started raising Cocker Spaniels. For the better part of a decade, he seemed always to have a new litter of Cockers in his backyard, where he'd built a makeshift kennel. The Cockers turned out to be good bird dogs—especially for quail and for pheasant. The most famous of Gramps' Cockers he dubbed Stupido Tiger, legendarily the best pheasant dog Gramps or his friends had ever seen.

If there was no room for talk of love in Dad's and Gramps' narratives about how they felt about dogs, it was clear that their sentiment ran deep. They both pooh-poohed the idea of loving a dog and spoke about dogs as though they held a purely utilitarian function, like a good pair of hiking boots, a jeep or a gun. But reading Dad's wartime letters to Gramps led me to think of their dogs as emotional conduits through which father and son could express softer sentiments for each other—love that perhaps could not be expressed easily in a direct way.

When I was living with Gramps, after Dad's death, he asked me if I remembered Dad's dog-calling whistle. I sure did. Dad called his dogs with a singular, somewhat mournful-sounding whistle on a minor chord that consisted of four short high-pitched bursts, followed by a fifth that started on the same note as the first four, but then dropped down half an octave.

I did the whistle for Gramps: "TWEE-TWEE-TWEE-TWEE-TWEEeeee"

Gramps smiled and said, "Yep, that's the one. When your Dad was in college, he had summer jobs where he wouldn't get home until late. I'd stay awake in bed—couldn't sleep until I heard him come in the back gate, and he'd whistle for the dogs. It's a funny thing, ya know, but when your Dad was overseas during the war, sometimes in the evening, I swear I could hear him in the backyard, whistling for the dogs."

○

If there was a Canine Hunting Hall of Fame in the Messner family, it ended well before my time, with Gramps' champion hunter Stupido Tiger. All of the dogs I knew were hunting failures, including our first dog, Lady. Springer Spaniels aren't known as "good deer hounds," but they do have reputations as great bird dogs. Dad trained Lady at home in the back yard to find and retrieve quail and pheasant wings. When she was old enough to go pheasant hunting, Dad took her to his friend Fred Jacobs' ranch. According to the story he would later tell, Dad and Lady walked down to a small body of water. Dad raised and fired his shotgun over the dog once and only once. On hearing the blast, Dad said, "she turned tail and ran for it, straight back to Fred's place and hid under a bed."

After that, Lady was gun shy, cowering at the mere sight of a rifle or a shotgun. As a family dog, she was valued by all of us, but as a hunting dog, she was useless.

Tiger also turned out to be a dud. Brittany Spaniels were known as good bird dogs, and I hoped that Tiger would be able to go out quail hunting with Dad, Gramps and me. I cut the wings off of some quail we'd shot in Chualar Canyon, and tried to train Tiger with them. Dad taught me to first get Tiger acquainted with the smell of the wings, then to hide them in the yard and send the dog looking for them. If he returned with one, I was to shower him with praise and reward him with a dog biscuit. It didn't work. Tiger seemed to like the smell of the quail wings, but when I'd send him searching for them in the back yard, he'd inevitably return happily with Pokey the Turtle in his mouth.

Tiger proclaimed, through mom's ventriloquism, "I'm a lover, not a fighter."

Nor was Tiger a hunter. He was a fully domesticated dog. Sometimes I'd put a t-shirt on him, tucked in to a pair of my tighty-whitey underwear, and send him scampering through the house, his cropped tail wagging nervously through the leg-opening of the underwear. "God, kid," he'd say in his telltale whiny voice, "I don't see how you wear these damned things all the time!"

○

Shortly after Dad died, Mom gave me a small bit of money. When I was a baby, Dad had opened a bank account into which he'd automatically deposited two dollars a month. He'd done the same for Terry and for Linny. My amount turned out to be a few hundred dollars. With it, I bought four new tires for my car, and a Springer Spaniel puppy. For many years, I'd held a warm image of Lady in my memory. A month or so before she disappeared, I'd sat on the ground in the doorway of my parents' garage watching the cars roll by, my spindly legs spread toward the street. Lady sprawled calmly over my legs, spilling across both sides of my lap as I stroked her soft fur. This was my main memory of this dog that disappeared when I was six—a calm, cuddly, loving dog.

I wanted to get a Springer, a female like Lady. I'd just moved with my girlfriend Judith into a rented Sacramento house with an enclosed yard—perfect for a dog. We found a breeder who had a litter of Springers he was selling "without papers," so my dog was affordable, only fifty bucks.

I briefly considered calling my new dog Lady. But then I remembered the debacle of Tiger II, my last attempt to name a puppy after a beloved dog of my past. That hadn't worked out so well. And besides, Dad had often said that he didn't consider it a good thing to have been named Russell Jr., after his dad. To differentiate him from Russell Sr., his family routinely called him "Hank," a nickname Dad despised. "Everybody deserves to start fresh with his own name," Dad proclaimed.

I figured the same might be true for dogs. But I wasn't sure what to name this new pup. Judith and I decided to get loaded and brainstorm some names. Following a pipe-load of Northern California Green, we decided it was suitable—hilariously so—that the dog's full name would be English Muffin With Butter and Honey. Muffy, for short.

The Muff, as I came to call her, was spirited (others had stronger words for her hyperkinetic style), and I did little to temper her frantic energies. I was at the height of my Rousseauian, Summervillian, anarchistic "let our natures unfold unfettered by authoritarian training" phase. I extended this philosophy to my puppy. Subsequently, Muffy never learned not to jump all over each visitor to the house. She was remarkably unresponsive when I pleaded with her to "mellow out," though she did eventually learn not to pee on the carpet. When I extended a tennis ball above my head, she would bounce repeatedly like a yo-yo on a string, her long ears flapping like Dumbo's, until I'd throw the ball.

The Muff's frenetic energy was both a joy to behold and a shocking revelation, given my memories of placid Lady. My mom reminded me that Lady had been six years old already when I was born, and twelve when I'd

Michael A. Messner

The Muff and I (1977).

had that calm and memorable moment with her on my lap. "Muffy'll calm down in a year or two," Mom assured me.

My vet told me that two years was the point at which she'd start to settle down. A Springer owner I met at the park one day shook her head and told me it'd be more like four years.

The Muff never did calm down. Her forte was retrieving Frisbees I'd toss repeatedly into a river, the ocean, or a swimming pool. And she was fixated especially on fetching tennis balls. Pretty much anywhere we went, Muffy would embark on a ball-hunt, unsystematically but doggedly zigzagging across a yard or a field, her nose to the ground like a divining rod, her cropped tail zip-zip-zipping back and forth, until somehow she would zero in on some long-lost grimy tennis ball. The Muff would proceed to add her own saliva to whatever foul crud already coated the ancient ball. She'd then joyfully flip it into someone's clean lap and back off a couple of steps to begin her insistent pogo until her unwilling mark threw the ball.

I told my friends and family—only half-jokingly—that The Muff was The Greatest Dog Who Ever Lived. I came to love her partly, I'm sure, because I felt her to be a final gift to me from Dad. For the next twelve years, Muffy was with me everywhere, through transitions major and minor: in Sacramento with Judith, through our break-up; in my Corolla on a cross-country summer trek to Colorado; back to Salinas where we lived for a few months with Mom; on to Santa Cruz living for six months in a tiny dive so close to the Beach and Boardwalk you could hear the rumble of the "Giant Dipper" roller-coaster; off to Oakland to live with Granny and Gramps as I started grad school (The Muff adding life—and fleas—to the house); then after Gramps' death to live in a former mortuary, a low-ceilinged downstairs flat, where they used to store the stiffs, in the flatlands of Berkeley. There, I had no back door, and the Muff would simply dive in and out of the open window to go outside to pee. In this place I came to believe that The Muff and I shared a telepathic bond—I would transmit ideas and feelings to her, and she'd hear, understand and respond (this worked best, to be sure, when I was plenty stoned). From there, we moved to a little house on a hill in El Cerrito, where Pierrette and I began our lives together (here, sadly, The Muff was demoted, no longer welcome to drink from the toilet); and finally to Los Angeles, where Pierrette and I bought our first home, the home in which Miles and Sasha were born.

In L.A., The Muff slipped into old age and became progressively blind. But she never fully "calmed down," as promised. Until nearly the end, The Muff navigated our back yard confidently, like a blind person reading Braille, tail zipping back and forth, in a never-ending search for a tennis ball. When finally I could see that she was in pain, and especially when she no longer showed any interest in a tennis ball, I knew it was time to put her down.

It was two days before Christmas in 1990, and we were about to drive to Northern California to join up with Pierrette's and my families. That morning, I carried The Muff into the vet's office in my arms, stroked her fur, kissed her, thanked her gently for everything, and handed her over. I climbed back into my car, and lowered my head on to the steering wheel, crying full sobs. Then, as I thought of Pierrette and little Miles waiting for me at home, I heard Dad's voice: "Ready to go inside now?" I took a couple of deep breaths, and said aloud, "Yeah, I guess so." I started the engine and drove the few blocks home to pick up Pierrette and Miles, and we headed up the I-5 to be with our families.

○

In the spring of 2009, Mom and I drove from Salinas to the North Bay Area town of Petaluma to visit my sister Terry, who had been institutionalized for over a year. Six years earlier, in her mid-fifties, Terry was diagnosed with early onset Alzheimers. For the next few years, as her memory and her identity gradually deserted her, she quit her job, sold her home, and lived variously with both of her adult sons, until they could no longer care for her. During those years, when I would see her or talk with her on the phone, she would invariably tell me "my girls"—meaning her two dogs—"are what keep me going. They really take care of me; they love me."

For years, Terry had a succession of dogs, always two at a time, staggered in age so that when the senior one died, the younger one, now middle-aged, could initiate the younger dog Terry would get from the pound. One of the first signs that Terry was losing her memory was when she started getting lost while walking her dogs in her own neighborhood. The dogs, she said, would lead her back to her home. When it became apparent that she would need institutional care, the misery of this idea was largely about being separated from her beloved dogs.

On that visit in 2009, Mom and I sat next to sixty-one-year old Terry in her wheelchair, Mom lovingly feeding her chips of dark chocolate, combing her hair, creaming her hands and talking to her as Terry babbled words that made little sense and looked at us with what seemed to me no sense of recognition. Routinely, as we spoke to her ("Eric and Adam, your sons love you, Terry. This is Mike: I love you, Terry"), her right hand would reach out from her wheelchair, stroking the air as close to the ground as she could reach, seeking something furry she could caress, some comfort, I assume, from her dogs. Terry could no longer remember who I am, but it seems that her beloved dogs were still deeply imprinted in her mind.

I told her, "Apollo loves you, Terry. Lady loves you, and Ripley loves you."

Her watery eyes looked directly into mine, and I imagined a moment of connection.

6
Stout-Hearted Men

I perched on the edge of my bed, hoping I'd get lucky. It was August 5, 1971, and I sat alone, fully attentive to the matter-of-fact voice of the radio announcer, as he called out this year's Selective Service Draft Lottery numbers. One by one, he would announce the birth date of each young man born in 1952, and then pull a number between 1 and 365 from a drum. These random numbers were then used to determine which eighteen- and nineteen-year-old guys would be drafted into the Army: high number, you were safe; low number, your head was shaved and you were off to 'Nam. I knew that in due course this disembodied voice would call a number that, arbitrarily married to my birth date, would alter the trajectory of my life in immeasurable ways. Fidgeting, I awaited the verdict.

The Vietnam War was winding down. Recently, Nixon's "Vietnamization" of this by-then unpopular war had been shifting the burden of the conflict away from U.S. soldiers. The previous year, 1970, the number of American troops who had been shipped home in coffins—a few more than 6000—had shrunk to half the number who had been killed in 1969. And thus far in 1971, the number of American troops in Vietnam, and the U.S. casualty count, had continued to decline. Still, the flag-shrouded coffins I saw on the TV news looked to me like a lot of dead young guys. I didn't want to be one of them.

I had drifted through my mid-teens obliviously cocooned in a sweet suburban haze. Although I was vaguely aware of the passionate national argument for and against the war, I was pretty much ignorant of the terms of the debate. Despite the national turmoil, I really hadn't thought that much about the war, obsessed as I was with more important things—basketball and girls. But I knew I didn't want to join the military. Not for any good political reason, though—it just seemed, well, inconvenient.

Until then, I'd been unmindful of the searing anti-war critiques of Bob Dylan, Joan Baez and even John Lennon. But when I heard Country Joe and the Fish sing "Be the first one on your block to have your boy come home in a box," the dangers of this war smacked me like a ton of napalm. And despite my ignorance of the politics of the war, one piece of information was crystal clear: the gradual ramping down of U.S. ground troops in Vietnam meant that today, only those young men who were unlucky enough to draw low lottery numbers—say, below 100—would end up getting drafted into the Army.

The announcer said "July first," my birthday. I clenched my fists atop my knees, closed my eyes and held my breath through the short pause. His next words, "284" jolted through me like an electrical charge. I leapt vertically, screaming "Yes!" my hands striking the ceiling.

I sprinted through the house to tell Dad, but halfway through the kitchen I stopped in my tracks. How would Dad actually feel about this? Was it possible he'd be disappointed? After all, during the previous year he'd gently prodded me to join NROTC. Dad reasoned that if I joined the Navy, rather than waiting to be drafted into the Army, it was far less likely I'd be sent to fight in Vietnam. I told him I'd think about it, all the while biding my time, hoping it all would just go away.

I slowed to a walk, came into Dad's room and announced as calmly as I could, so as not to betray my glee that I'd gotten a high lottery number, that I was almost assured not to be drafted.

Dad nodded and gave me a playful slap on the shoulder: "Well, I guess Gramps fought in a war and I fought in a war, so maybe it's time that it skips a generation."

That was that. Dad seemed relieved, but it was also clear that I should not make a big deal out of this. After all, he was still a Captain in the U. S. Naval Reserve. He supported the war and had no patience for protestors. I was still a year away from the political awakening that would lead me to take an active anti-war stand. But on this day, the lucky number 284 slammed the door on military service and allowed me to focus back on basketball and girls.

○

Gramps got especially grumpy around Veterans Day. I couldn't figure it out: he had fought in World War I and for decades had been an active member of the Veterans of Foreign Wars. On the morning of Veteran's Day in 1980, Gramps sat with his breakfast—a cup of watery coffee, a piece of burnt toast slathered with orange marmalade, and a single slice of cold liverwurst. I tried to cut through his cranky mood by wishing him happy Veterans Day. Big mistake.

"*Veterans* Day!" he barked at me with the gravelly voice of the life-long smoker. "It's not *Veterans* Day. It's *Armistice* Day! Those...gawd...damned... *politicians...changed* it to Veterans Day. After they kept getting us into more wars."

Gramps was hyperventilating now, his liverwurst forgotten.

"Buncha' *crooks!* They don't fight the wars, ya know. Guys like me fight the wars. We called it 'The war to end all wars.' And we *believed* it!—*Veterans* day!"

The Armistice had been signed on the eleventh hour of the eleventh day, on the eleventh month of 1918, but Gramps was one of the unlucky Doughboys who had to stay six months longer in Russia, as part of a counterrevolutionary U.S.-British force that tried and failed to defeat the Soviet Red Army. In the years following his return home, Armistice Day symbolized to Gramps the end of war, and the hope of a lasting peace. Veterans day was a slap in the face: hope evaporated, replaced with the ugly reality that politicians would continue to find reasons to send American boys to fight and die in wars.

When I was a little boy and I would sit with Gramps in his den, he would occasionally tell stories of The Great War, but like many veterans of his generation, he didn't like to talk about it. Mostly I had to read between the lines to get much information, and the artifacts he pulled out of his gun cabinet offered tantalizing glimpses. A small scrap of paper, signed by a British Officer read: "Transport Officer: Please supply bearer with 3 sleighs for the purpose of moving material to burn Kitza 10:III:19."

The sleighs, Gramps told me, were pulled by reindeer across snow and frozen lakes, and were filled with canisters of gasoline, that were used to burn down the Russian town of Kitza as the U.S. troops retreated. Nearly breathless with excitement, I asked him, "Did you ever kill anyone in the war?"

Gramps survived his WW I stint in frigid Northern Russia (1918-1919).

He snorted disapprovingly at the question, paused, and then told me a funny story: "We had no running water, and one night I woke up so thirsty. So I got up, and drank from a puddle of rainwater in the middle of a dirt road. The next morning, in the daylight, the puddle had a big pile of horse manure in it."

I wanted more, but I think he knew I attached a false sense of glory and excitement to war. For Gramps, war was freezing your ass off, drinking water with horseshit in it, and praying every day to get out of the nightmare, back home safely. The rest, I think, was unspeakable, except in coded, humorous snapshots.

The Polar Bears—as they were sometimes called due to their ability to endure the extreme cold of this Russian post above the Arctic Circle—skirmished with Bolshevik forces for several months after the Armistice. In 1973, the VFW Magazine that Gramps subscribed to ran a story about the U.S. Expeditionary Forces with whom he had been sent to Russia. Gramps thought the article lacked detail, so he hand-wrote a reply, which Mom then typed for him and sent in to the magazine.

> *Guard Duty at night was a nightmare. We had fur hats with reversible black and white linings, tied under the chin. Coats were with high sheepskin collars and at 40 degrees below zero your breath froze the hat, fur collar and your beard into a piece of ice. You had to sit in front of a roaring fire before you could get your clothes off. One hour of guard duty was all you could take.*
>
> *Another experience I remember was the ride across the Dvina River to Archangel by reindeer, while it was frozen over. A kind of taxi service, operated by Laplanders. The driver stood on the sleigh runner, you sat inside, and with a series of grunts to the pony, away you went.*

What Gramps didn't hint at in this letter was whom he was gliding across the ice to visit in Archangel. But he told me once, as we sat at his desk scrutinizing his treasures. Gramps unfolded a narrow ribbon of thinly transparent paper that was neatly folded in the tattered leather wallet he'd carried through the war. On it was typed, "Pvt. Messner, R. J. has permission to be absent from his organization till 11:00 p.m. May 19, 1919 to visit Archangel." He'd kept five of these tiny passes to Archangel, their dates spanning May and June of 1919. Holding one of them between thumb and forefinger, gazing at it, Gramps told me in a quiet voice, "There was a girl I visited there."

He didn't tell me her name or any more about their relationship. But in the tiny notebook Gramps carried through the war, presented to him by The Walther League, the Lutheran youth group he'd belonged to at home, a few Russian words were jotted in pencil, including what appears to be a name, Rubena Kruetihke, marked phonetically perhaps to help Gramps pronounce it correctly. And directly below this name is written 31-17-38. What, I wondered?—Rubena Kruetihke's phone number? Her measurements?

There was this Russian girl over there, but Gramps also knew that back home Ruth Paynter waited for his return. While he was away in Russia, Ruth and her parents had left the failing mines and mills of Michigan and moved to the promised land of Berkeley, California. For the duration of the war, Gramps also kept in his wallet a photo of Ruth and him, taken before the war, on July 4, 1917. Perhaps he had received this photo enclosed with a letter from Ruth, because on its back he wrote: "September, 1918 in Tigra, Russia, 'My Darling Pet'".

In Gramps' gun cabinet, tucked into a flower-patterned cloth bag with a drawstring, were several letters he had received from home during the war. Most were from family members, full of newsy snapshots of the home front and prayerful wishes for the safe return of their "soldier boy." Don and Doba—Gramps' nicknames for the aunt and uncle who raised him—wrote in a letter dated October 15, 1918:

> *Well Russell we expect that you are over in Russia. Don said he is sure you are over there. It was in the paper that the 310th Engrs, made up of Michigan and Wisc troops were in Russia. My but it is a terribly far way. It sure is close to the end of the world. Just think how far we are apart. But the Lord can protect you there as well as right here at home, and we do pray for Him to do so... I hope you are dressed good and warm Russ. It is awful to think of that you aren't warmly dressed...There is an epidemic of influenza in this state. The camps are full of it. Thousands died of it and a whole lot more sick. There were a number of boys brought home dead. Tompin boy of Lake Linden and Hosking of Hubbel.*

Like many letters from home this one included an offhand comment about hunting.

> *Ameil is going hunting pretty regular now. He got a nice boat. He said he wishes you were home to go with him. Ameil crossed the lake and brought home with a rabbit one time.*

And Don and Doba signaled to Russell that there was much riding on his safe return.

I got a letter from Ruth. She said she writes to you every day. She sure is some lonesome. Poor girl her whole future depends on you Russ. How grand it will be if ever you get back home once again. Oh what a grand greeting all those dear boys will get.

The letter was signed:

With all our love from Don and Doba, who think of you every moment of the day xxxxx

By July 1919, Russ was in Brest, France. Here was taken the large panoramic photo that Gramps would later hang in his Oakland den, and which now hangs in my study, of he and the 213 other survivors of Company A of the U.S. Army's 310th Engineers. The United States had lost over 100,000 soldiers in this terrible war—many of them to the flu epidemic that killed millions worldwide. Gramps was among the lucky ones, his only scrape an emergency appendectomy in a Russian field hospital. On July 25, 1919, Gramps received his Honorable Discharge in Camp Grant, IL. The discharge papers certified that Russell Messner had received no citations, medals, decorations, badges, or wounds in service. It said that he had no particular marksmanship gunner qualifications, and under "horsemanship," he was listed as "not mounted." His physical condition was determined to be "good," and his character was judged "Excellent." In short, he had served his country with no particular distinction, and had survived.

Gramps had spent ten months in Northern Russia—six of them after the Armistice—and he told me years later that it was so miserable there, "I wondered sometimes if it would ever end."

Once he was home, things happened quickly. He followed Ruth to Berkeley, where they married on January 26, 1920. Granny and Gramps built their family without delay. Russell Jr. was born less than nine months later, on October 10, 1920. A daughter Dorothea arrived nine months after that.

Michael A. Messner

After the war, Granny and Gramps started their family in Berkeley (1922).

Gramps' Army discharge papers listed "mining" as the one vocation he knew. This would do him little good in Berkeley. By 1922, he had secured an apprenticed position in a skilled trade, with Traung Label and Lithograph, later to be called Schmidt Lithograph. He started at $21.00 a week, with a contract that assured him that after six months of satisfactory work, his salary would be raised $2.00 per week. The deal included an employer-paid life insurance policy worth $500 to his survivors, and a provision that if he stayed with Traung for at least four years, he would get a $100 bonus. He lasted the four years and more. Every weekday morning until the day he retired, Gramps took the train from his home in Oakland to the ferryboat that would take him across the Bay to his job in San Francisco. In May of 1937, Gramps and Granny purchased the home that they would live in for the rest of their lives. They secured a loan for the amount of $5600, at 5% interest. Gramps kept the Amortization Schedule in his gun cabinet. Each month for the next fifteen years, he would set the Schedule on his desk and pencil a straight line through that month's payment–which began at $48.91 a month—until the house was paid off. By April 1, 1952, three months before my birth, Granny and Gramps owned outright the home at 5905 Claremont Avenue.

○

Dad was marching in the living room and singing at the top of his lungs. It was a late afternoon in 1960, and Mom had just purchased a spiffy reel-to-reel tape recorder—a blonde mahogany model, designed to look like an elegant modern end table. Mom bought the machine mostly to record and play all of her favorite music, and in the coming years, our house hummed constantly with the crooning of Frank Sinatra, Perry Como, Johnny Mathis, and the jazzy tunes of Herb Alpert and the Tijuana Brass. The recorder also had a microphone, and Mom would pull it out now and then and encourage us kids to tell a story or sing a song. On this day, Linny had just sung Waltzing Matilda when Dad walked in the door, home from school. At first, Mom had to coax him to sing his favorite World War II song, "C'mon, Sweetie—'Give Me Some Men!'"

Finally, he got into it: feet stomping in place, fists pumping, chin up, Dad belted out the song we'd heard him sing so many times.

> *Give me some men who are stout-hearted men*
> *And I'll soon give you ten thousand more.*
> *Shoulder to shoulder and bolder and bolder*

> *They grow as they go to the fore!*
> *Oh! There's nothing in this world can halt or mar our plan,*
> *When stout-hearted men can get together man to man!*

The way Dad sang this song—especially the overly-dramatized way he belted out the final line: "*Whenaaah*, Stout-hearted *Menaaah*, can get together *Maahn* to *Maahn*!"—left us all in stitches. His tone and comportment were hilariously self-mocking, yet still somehow reverent. I laughed along with everyone when Dad sang this song. But to my eight-year-old ears, the song's words—especially the idea of ten thousand unstoppable stout-hearted men, shoulder to shoulder, bolder and bolder, saving the world from tyranny—kindled in me a deep sense of awe. I idolized Dad and all of the men who had won this war, men who later would be called "The Greatest Generation."

○

In the late 1930's, as Europe once again plunged into war, Gramps joined with veterans organizations that were urging the United States to stay out of the war, to remain neutral. Gramps kept in his gun cabinet a single magazine page, glued to a piece of cardboard. The page was a Memorial Day 1937 VFW position paper on war and peace. It presented evidence that the U.S. government had joined the fighting in World War I partly out of the pursuit of profit for rich industrialists. It declared that "The Veterans of Foreign Wars of the United States was the first veteran organization to incorporate a militant demand for neutrality," and encouraged its membership to pressure the U.S. Congress to stick to the VFW platform of "Peace for America." World War I veterans were especially urged to lead the country in making "…a solemn pledge that the sacrifices of our hero dead were not made in vain."

The history of World War II that I learned in school was a story of a country fully united against fascism, with the exception perhaps of a few unpatriotic anarchists who were swept aside and thrown in jail. I would never have known that one of the most patriotic organizations in the nation—the VFW—actively opposed the U.S. entry into the war if Gramps hadn't told me. The fact that he saved this mounted page declaring his organization's commitment to peace and neutrality shows how heartfelt his feelings were. And it wasn't simply politics underlying Gramps' anti-war stance; this was a deeply personal matter as well. With a teenaged son at home, he told me years later, he prayed that his country would not once again go to war.

As a college student at Cal, Dad had joined the Navy ROTC. A year after the Japanese attack on Pearl Harbor, he was called for service. He shipped out for training in Chicago on April 26, 1943, before he could attend his college graduation. Briefly home, he married his college sweetheart Betty on August 28, and two days later he was off to San Diego. On October 8, he boarded the U.S.S. Polk, arriving a few days later in Pearl Harbor. For the next fourteen months, he would ship back-and-forth from Pearl Harbor to South Pacific islands freshly wrenched away from the Japanese by the U.S. Marines: Tarawa in The Gilbert Islands, Eniwetok in the Marshalls, and Ulithi in the Carolines.

When Dad shipped out to the South Pacific just shy of his 23rd birthday, he was close to the same age Gramps had been when he was called to war. But unlike his father, Ensign Russell Messner, Jr. was a college-educated officer, put in charge of a group of enlisted men. Immediately after the Marines would take an island, the Navy would come in, move materials on to the beach and establish the beginnings of a base. As the Beachmaster, Dad was in charge of this activity. Once, when I was a kid, Linny announced at dinner that her teacher had asked everybody to say what their dads had done during the war. She proudly told her class that her dad had been a beachcomber. Dad burst into laughter, and Mom said, "No, no, honey: Daddy was a beach*master!*"

Being a Navy Beachmaster was not a front-line battle job, but it was substantially more important and certainly more dangerous than beachcombing. Like Gramps, Dad did not like to talk about his war. I probed to find out if Dad had seen any combat, and he said no, that he considered himself very lucky never to have been in the midst of fighting. But when he landed on islands not long after the fighting had ceased, he'd seen some terrible things, he said, awful things done to human beings.

Dad (above right in t-shirt) with his Stout-Hearted Men somewhere in the South Pacific (1944).

Once, Dad told me, they found that two Japanese soldiers had been hiding in the water, directly under the very dock that he had stood on for two days, as he supervised the landing and unloading of materials. This story haunted me—I obsessed over the image of these two armed men hiding just a few feet below Dad. I imagined grenades, fixed bayonets, a bonzai suicide strike.

I asked him, "Did the Japs try to attack you? Did you have to kill them?"

"No, the *Japanese* were scared and cold," he said. "They just came out and gave themselves up."

It hadn't occurred to me that these treacherous enemies might have been two frightened men, shivering with cold. And I was struck by how Dad emphasized *"Japanese,"* his tone scolding by implication my use of the term "Japs." I wonder now: Dad was a lifelong Californian, and by this time he was a teacher in Salinas. A substantial number of the boys who played on his football and basketball teams were Japanese-American kids who had been raised in wartime American concentration camps. This was something nobody talked about during my childhood—even my Japanese-American friends in school. But I suspect Dad was sensitive to the humiliations that had been visited upon his fellow citizens during the war.

○

While he was in The South Pacific, Dad wrote two sets of letters home. One set was intended for Gramps, Granny, his sister Dorothea and wife Betty, who was living with Granny and Gramps. The second set of letters was intended only for Gramps' eyes. More than once in these letters Dad warned Gramps, "Now don't tell the women this…" For the rest of his life, Gramps kept these letters bundled in his gun cabinet; I hold them now in my hands, these hand-written dispatches, connecting a son to a father who will understand what he is going through. From Eniwitok on April 4, 1944, Dad wrote to Gramps.

Hi there old timer! How's the world treating you these days. Boy I sure envy you, you have a whole house full of beautiful women, & I haven't even seen one for nigh on to 3 months now. Some guys get all the breaks.

It sure is tough out here at times—oh, I don't mean physically, it's the separation from Her, & everything & everybody that means so much to you. I guess I don't need to tell you about that, do I Dad? I'm very thankful that I have never had to go thru what you did Dad. I know I have had it easy, compared to you & I thank God for it, cause I know it is an answer to one of your prayers, as well as mine. I can always remember—ever since I was a little kid—you always said—"Son, I pray God that you never have to go thru what I did." As yet, I haven't, I'm sure, & the way things are shaping up now Dad it doesn't look like I will ever have to. Don't know just yet what is going to become of us—we are just marking time out here now—waiting I guess.

While Dad was away at war, Gramps continued to hunt and fish with his friends, as he prayed for his son's safe return. And for the son, far away on some small island in the South Pacific, to dream of hunting with his father offered a major touchstone for their connection. In one of his first letters, dated September 28, 1943, in the middle of deer season and just before he shipped out from San Diego to Pearl Harbor, Dad wrote:

Hi old timer! How goes it with 'ye olde' hunt this year. Sure hope you connected, Dad. More than once I have thought of you this past week. In fact there hasn't been a day pass when I haven't thot of you & wished I was there to help you clean him. –Optimistic, no?? Well even if you didn't get one I know you have had a swell time, & that's what really counts. Well Dad with Italy down for the count, maybe it won't be too long before we can make it together again…Please write me a day-by-day account of your trip will you Dad? Make it a series of letters if you wish, but don't leave out anything. I sure wish I could have been with you.

Hunting was a recurring theme in Dad's letters to Gramps. On April 23, 1944 the day he boarded a Navy LST to ship out of Eniwitok to Pearl Harbor, Dad conspiratorially noted his having spirited away a special Carbine rifle and a sleeping bag that would come in handy for future hunting trips with Gramps.

Well Dad, I am not in a position to get you anything for you birthday so I decided to write you a letter—that's the least I can do for such a swell Dad. I've got a brand new Carbine put away for you back at the base, so if I can ever bring that thru the customs office, we'll be set for Lake County. Two days ago I "obtained" one of the most beautiful sleeping bags you have ever laid your eyes on. It is practically brand new, is water proof, very light & is a zipper bag. If I can get that home it will really be something.

King of the Wild Suburb

Overseas, Dad "obtained" the Carbine that, two decades later, I would hunt with (1944).

Michael A. Messner

On September 16, 1944, a few days before shipping out of Pearl Harbor on the USS Typhoon for a six-week stint on the Caroline Island of Ulithi, Dad updated Gramps about his clandestine plan.

About the carbine, well I haven't gotten up quite enough nerve to send one of those home as yet. That's really supposed to be forbidden! I know a fellow who sent one home, but it hasn't arrived as yet, so I'm waiting to see how he makes out...Sure wish I could be home with you dad to go along and pack that buck for you. Be good now, and good luck to you on your trip Dad, boy how I wish I could be there to go along. I pray that this whole business will be over a year from now, it could be you know, very easily, but I doubt it.

Dad dreamed that the Carbine—a compact semi-automatic weapon designed for combat—would neatly convert to peacetime hunting, just as he would. Two decades later the Carbine rested in the gun rack in Gramps' den, where it became the most important weapon in my fantasy arsenal, and the first rifle I would carry on a deer hunt.

Now sporting the two stripes of a Lieutenant, Dad returned to the mainland just in time for Gramps' and Granny's 25th wedding anniversary party in January, 1945. It was a joyous affair. A photo of the entire party posing around a beaming Granny and Gramps shows Dad wearing his formal Navy blues, a strained smile on his face. A stern-faced Betty stands beside him, arms crossed tightly across her chest. They barely kept up appearances for the anniversary party, but their marriage was over. While still overseas dreaming of his return, Dad had received a "Dear John" letter from Betty, who had been living in Granny and Gramps' home and partying with other men. Years later, the one time I broached the topic with Gramps he shook his head, "I could see the kind of woman she was."

Dad and Betty divorced. By the end of January, Dad was stationed in Chicago, where he began to date LaVerne Raab. He liked LaVerne, but when she invited him home to meet her family, Russ fell truly in love—with LaVerne's younger sister Anita.

Anita Raab was a gorgeous wartime U.S.O. worker, who had done some modeling work for local magazines and newspapers. Anita and Russ fell madly in love, and were married in Chicago—with sister LaVerne standing up for Anita.

Dad was discharged from active duty on May 13 1946, five months after V-J Day. He and Mom were married on Oct. 19, 1946 at Mom's Congregational Church in Elmhurst, Illinois. With the war over, the

young

Mom and Dad, newlyweds (1946).

couple moved to Oakland, and lived with Gramps and Granny while Dad completed his teaching credential at Cal. My parents were modest contributors to the baby boom. I recall Dad telling me that when the war ended, he felt that he was "kind of behind, making up for lost time."

Terry was born August, 1947, and a month later Dad started his job at Salinas High School, 100 miles south of where he was born and raised. Linny would be born three years later, and I showed up in 1952.

○

My wars were all fantasies. As a child, I vanquished invading Krauts from the upstairs window of Gramps' den, and battled Mexican soldiers in his back yard, wearing my Davy Crockett outfit. Back home in Salinas, I strove to dominate the neighborhood arms race. I built my personal arsenal of toy rifles and machine guns, topped by a real army helmet that mom bought for me at the Army Surplus Store. I felt just like John Wayne.

For my eighth birthday in 1960, I received a plastic spring-loaded mortar, its barrel the size of my arm that launched a six-inch long plastic bomb thirty feet across our front lawn. This, I figured, gave me the equivalent of the Guns of Navarone in my neighborhood. I was ready for Jon Scattini or Donnie Hallstone to attack from around the block, or, I imagined, for the Krauts, the Reds, or any other bad guys who might be foolish enough to threaten our placid neighborhood. As the 1960's commenced, the ubiquitous news of the Cold War arms race made it apparent to me that these kinds of threats were becoming very real.

○

In my dream, I am standing on the grassy infield of the Salinas High School track, surrounded by scores of kids and adults. Suddenly, a plane—a small prop-job—approaches from the west, flying so low it barely clears the tops of the houses and trees. I watch as it flies directly over us, slowing, its engine sputtering. It's going to crash, I realize. The plane manages to pass over us, dropping perilously lower, and as it disappears behind the high school buildings, its engine cuts out. There is a moment of absolute silence, as though everyone on the infield is holding their breath. Then, there is a massive explosion, and a mushroom cloud rises before my eyes.

King of the Wild Suburb

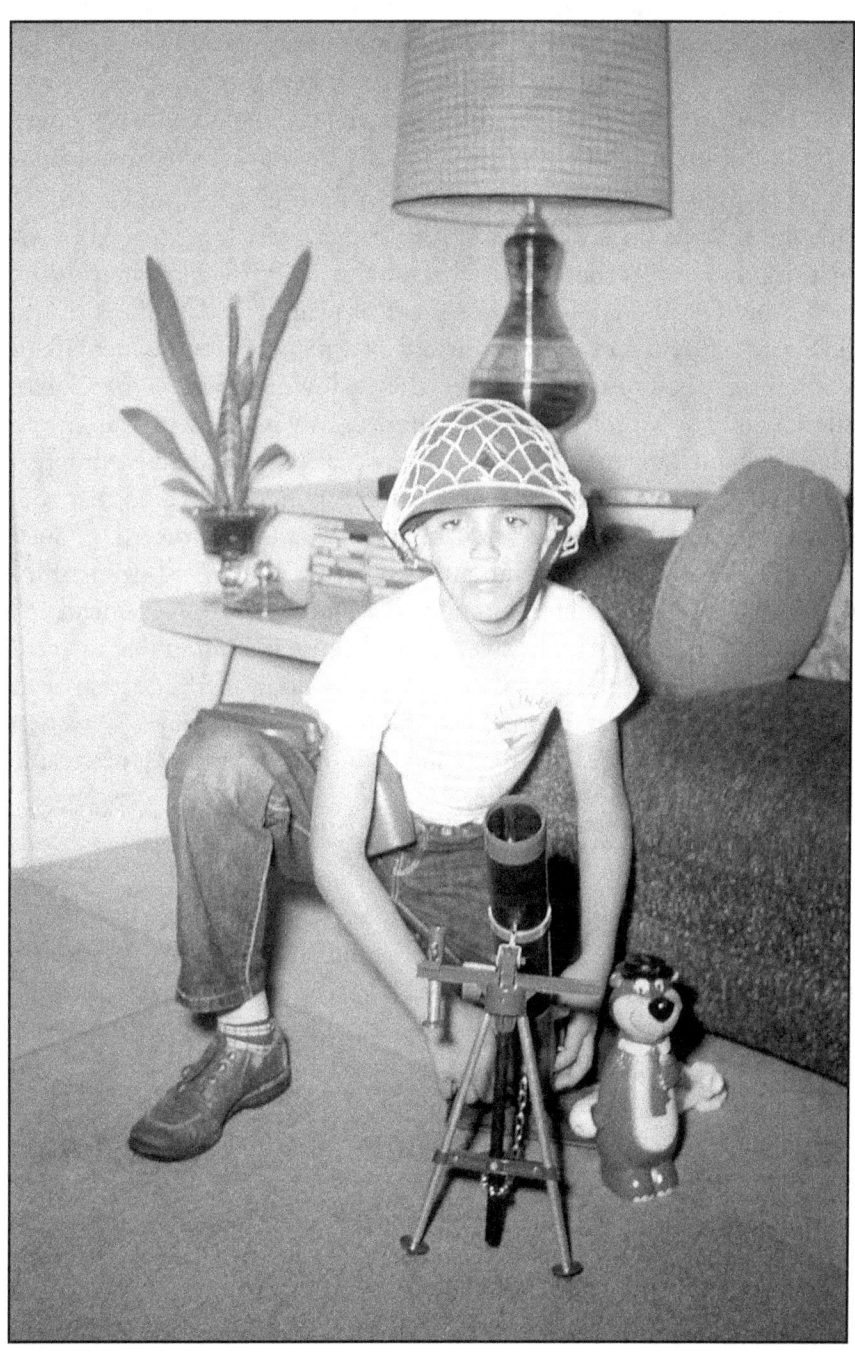

I felt smarter than the average defender of liberty (1960).

Michael A. Messner

I open my eyes, and I'm in my dark bedroom. It's totally quiet; everyone is asleep. Slivers of light play across the walls of my room as a lone car accelerates through the intersection in front of our corner home. Joe the deer stands sentry directly above my bed, his glass eyes surveying the room as always. I shiver and with both hands I clutch the green quilt with the pirate ships on it, pulling it up to my chin. I shut my eyes and go back to sleep.

My exploding airplane nightmare began around 1962, and it would continually intrude on my sleep for at least a decade. It's a typical Cold-War-Kid nightmare. At that time in the autumn of 1962—right after Willie Mays and my Giants had fallen just short of beating the Yankees in the World Series—President Kennedy squared off against Soviet Premier Nikita Krushchev for what turned out to be the real World Series, the Cuban Missile Crisis. I was pretty sure that the Russian missiles in Cuba were unable to reach California, but I also knew that bombs could be dropped from planes. It seemed that the teachers in my school expected that too. Along with the usual fire and earthquake drills, we were instructed in "duck and cover" drills for atomic bomb attacks. When you see a huge flash of light, we were told, it could be an atomic detonation. "Always remember," the narrator of the "Duck and Cover" civil defense film reminded us as we watched images of kids playing baseball in their schoolyard, "The flash of an atomic bomb can come at any time, no matter where you may be." When you see this flash, we were told, immediately drop to your knees, preferably under your desk, and cover your head.

This duck and cover drill is laughable today, and the film that was shown to Cold War-era kids like me is now popular entertainment on YouTube. But back then, these drills instilled in me a terrifying sense of inevitability about nuclear annihilation. People were building home bomb shelters, and there were public discussions—including on an episode of my favorite TV show *The Twilight Zone*—about the morality of excluding your neighbors from the safety of your shelter, once the bombs start to drop. It was kind of like the "Little Red Hen" story; if you plan ahead and do the work to protect your family with a shelter, then you deserve to survive, and perhaps others don't.

My family did not build a bomb shelter, and I didn't know anybody who did. So I knew that once it started raining atom bombs, I would be stuck with the "duck and cover" survival strategy. Once in 1962 I was playing on my front lawn with Dennis Cahoon, a somewhat older ruffian who lived down the street. Dennis pooh-poohed my genuine U.S. Navy flight helmet and the toy submachine gun—I called it my Tommy gun—that I proudly brandished.

Just then, a small plane flew overhead.

"Mike," Dennis said, "that looks like a Russian plane, and it's going to drop an atom bomb right on your head."

I looked up. In the event of an atomic explosion, I realized, my Tommy gun would melt right along with me. Even my mighty mortar would be useless. Suddenly terrified, I dropped my weapon and bolted into the house to duck and cover under Mom's coffee table. Behind me, Dennis Cahoon hooted with pleasure.

○

I stood at parade rest on the side of a dry grassy knoll in the full sunshine, my right hand holding the barrel of the upright Carbine, its stock resting on the ground. Dad had left me here a few minutes earlier, and told me to watch the facing hill for deer. I wasn't sure what I was supposed to do if a buck did come along—I was only ten, and though Dad now let me carry this rifle, he didn't yet allow me keep it loaded. I sat for a few minutes and quickly grew bored. As I fiddled with the Carbine Dad had brought home from the war, I imagined how efficient I would be in combat, rapid-firing the fifteen-shot semi-automatic, pop-pop-pop. Before I knew it, I was no longer on a Chualar Canyon deer hunt; I was a soldier, standing alone on a hill on some island in the South Pacific, ready to fight the Japanese.

I proceeded with what I imagined to be the proper military rifle corps drill—feet together, standing at rigid attention, I jerked the Carbine vertically a few inches in front of my face, froze it there with both hands for a two-count, twirled it in a tight circle, paused again, then spread my feet to shoulder's width, and as I lowered the stock of the rifle to the ground with my right hand, I placed my left hand behind my back. Looking smart, chin up, I suddenly noticed that I was not alone. As I had performed my routine, Charley Dake had appeared over the facing knoll, and was standing there laughing.

Later that evening, as we all sat in the cabin eating dinner, Charley told everybody what he'd seen me doing on the hill, and snorted, "Looks like Mike wants to join the Army."

Everybody laughed.

Gramps smiled thinly, and said to me with a serious tone, "That right, Mike?"

Red-faced, I said "I dunno."

Michael A. Messner

My Tommy gun and I would melt when the atomic bombs fell (circa 1961).

○

I sit in my car, and try through the open window to get a good photo of Miles and Sasha, standing on the busiest street corner of our town, holding up anti-war signs. It's 2005, two years after the U.S. invasion of Iraq escalated into a permanent state of war. Sasha holds up a sign that indicates how many people have thus far died in this war, and Miles' impolitic sign reflects his sense of humor: "Even My Mom Hates Bush." Miles and Sasha are two of maybe seven protestors on this Friday evening, exhorting the people of South Pasadena to honk their horns against the war. I have never been so proud of my sons.

Watching Miles and Sasha that evening, I recalled Gramps' dashed hopes in the late-1930's that the government would not send his son off to war. And I reflected on Dad's saying to me back in 1971 when I drew that lucky number 284, "Well, I guess Gramps fought in a war and I fought in a war, so maybe it's time that it skips a generation."

And I thought: *No. Not skip. Stop.* It wasn't enough for me to have lucked out, only to have my own sons have to pick up arms and go to war. I'm proud of what Gramps and Dad did in their wars; it shaped the kinds of men they became, created a clear transition for them into the adult world of work and family life, and served as a template for the lessons of manhood they taught me. I am equally proud of my sons as they take action against war, and I say along with them: *No Mas.* Not for us, not for anyone.

Michael A. Messner

7
Trophy Head

"Mike's First Buck Sept. 1967"

Dad wrote that on the back of a photo of Gramps and him, posing with my buck and me. I'd seen this picture before, but not this particular one with the inscription on the back, not until after Dad died.

I was fifteen years old. It was the final day of deer season, which is usually timed so that it ends before the rut, when the does go into heat, and bucks lose all sense of caution. On this morning, Gramps dropped Bob, Duffy, Dad and me on a ridge above the Esterbrook Flats. As the sounds of Gramps coaxing the jeep down the mountain faded, we discussed who would go where. It was decided that Dad and I would take the route to the right, while Duffy and Bob would swing in an arc to our left—a classic pincer maneuver. Not five minutes after we parted, as Dad and I wove our way through some sparse brush, we heard a crashing noise, and saw a sudden flash of brown slashing through the brush, thirty yards in front of us. We raised our rifles and then lowered them together.

"It's a doe," Dad whispered.

The words had barely left Dad's lips when the brush exploded again, and this time the flash of brown was preceded by a huge rack of antlers. Hell-bent for leather, head down, the buck was hot on the heels of the doe. Dad and I raised our rifles again, but he lowered his, and let me have the shot. My heart raced. I aimed for the heart, right above the shoulder, held my breath, squeezed the trigger and dropped the buck in his tracks.

"You got him," Dad said.

Heart pounding, I sprinted toward the spot where the buck had fallen—and stopped dead in my tracks ten feet away. I'd not made a perfect shot. Underestimating the buck's speed, I'd failed to lead him enough to connect with a perfect kill shot to the heart.

My bullet had blown out a fist-sized chunk of bloody flesh and backbone, just above the buck's pelvis. His hind legs were useless, but he was still very much alive, thrashing his antlers and struggling with his front legs to pull himself upright. As Dad and I stood before the buck, he suddenly stopped struggling. Up on his front legs and perfectly still, the buck stared at us. Having heard the shot, Bob and Duffy rushed into the clearing, Bob erupting in envy:

"Oh, my God! What a rack! Lucky!" Indeed, I could see that this was a trophy head, one that we'd certainly want to mount. And this was the problem.

As we looked at the still living deer, and he looked at us, Dad and Bob pondered aloud how to finish him off without spoiling the mount.

"Not too high on the neck," Bob instructed.

Dad asked if I wanted to do it, but by now, my adrenaline rush had shifted to nausea. I glanced quickly at the gory wound and then looked directly into the eyes of the animal that moments earlier was on a fever-pitched beeline for a doe's white tail. I knew that if this were a few weeks earlier, before rutting, this seasoned veteran of the wild would have been way too smart to show himself to us. He'd have laid low in the brush as we walked by, oblivious to his existence. It wasn't fair.

A few years earlier, while quail hunting, Dad had told me to be on the lookout for cottontail rabbits. Walking through a small clearing, what I thought was a rabbit suddenly squirted in front of me. In a reflex action, I swung my shotgun around and blasted the creature. When I walked up to it and discovered it was not a rabbit, but a still-quivering little squirrel, I started spontaneously to cry.

Dad approached, saw me crying and asked, "Are you all right?"

"Yeah," I sniffled, "but I thought it was a rabbit; I didn't mean to shoot a squirrel."

"It's okay," he said. "People eat squirrels, too."

I said "Oh," and felt foolish for crying, as we walked away and left the dead animal on the ground.

This time though, I was older. I'd shot a buck, and I'd be damned if I was going to start crying. But when Dad asked me again if I wanted to finish him off, all I could manage was a murmur, "No, I don't think so."

The buck exhaled a rumbling blast through his nostrils and struggled in vain to gain his feet one more time. Duffy, clearly unsettled that we were forcing the animal to suffer while we debated the best way to ensure a good mounted head, blurted with a breaking voice, "Well, *somebody* finish him off, *please!*"

Dad did, with a point-blank shot just below the neck.

Without a word, Dad handed me the hand-sharpened knife he carried in a leather scabbard on his belt. It was my kill; I knew it was my responsibility to field dress the buck. Kneeling in the grass next to the dead animal, with the knife's razor sharp tip I executed a long cut from just below the sternum to above the genitals.

"Not too deep now," Dad instructed. "Cut into the intestine and you'll have a mess."

Dad's knife slicing through the buck's hide and muscle made a ripping sound, like Mom's pinking shears cutting through tightly stretched fabric. I pulled open the stomach cavity, holding my breath to avoid gagging from the smell. This wasn't my first time; Dad had given me anatomy lessons in the past as we plunged our hands into the warm guts of a freshly-killed deer. We always retrieved the liver; it was, the men said, "good eatin'." The rest we left in a steaming pile on the ground. As I completed the ritual field dressing of my buck, finally wiping the blood from Dad's knife on a tuft of dry grass, an oddly detached feeling settled upon me.

Back at the cabin, I posed for photos with my buck draped over the hood of the jeep. Then we pulled the dead animal to the ground, and I posed with Gramps and Dad. I tried to put on a face of modest pride. I couldn't articulate what I really felt: triumphant accomplishment on the surface, mixed with a deep undercurrent of guilt. And shame—unspeakable shame for feeling guilty during this moment of manly triumph. Where this guilt came from, I had no idea. Surely I'd grown up in a family where killing and eating animals was normal; heck, celebrated. Maybe it went back to Mom's personification of our family dogs. Or maybe Disney's depiction of human hunters akin to evil Nazis murdering the innocent (and very humanized) mother of Bambi influenced me more deeply than I could ever know.

Michael A. Messner

I attempted a look of modest pride (1967).

I have looked at this photo scores of times—I've scanned it, Photoshopped it, blown it up on the computer screen, stared into the eyes of Dad, Gramps and me, searching for hints of the complicated emotional cross-currents of that moment. For Gramps and Dad, I believe this was a proud coming-of-age moment that connected them to me and to each other. For me, it was that too, but also something other, something unanticipated. I had imagined that moment many times—me, the great hunter, bagging a trophy head, making me the envy of the all of the men. And indeed, as we posed with the buck, Charley declared that this was the biggest buck anyone had taken out of Chualar Canyon in a decade. What my fantasy had not anticipated was the well of empathy that bubbled up within me, the sense of foul play that I felt in having shot this buck as he blindly pursued a mate, and my visceral disgust with the bloody mess of it all.

I have a pile of these kinds of photos in a file I call "dead deer": Gramps with teenaged Dad, rifles in hand, a dead buck draped across the hood of the car; Dad with his bloody knife, skinning a deer hanging from a tree limb; six-year-old me in a cowboy hat, gap-toothed and grinning on our front lawn, lifting the head of Dad's buck by its antlers. I've pondered what these photos mean, and on one level, it's simple: People tend to have full photo albums of their weddings, but few pictures of the mundane daily moments of their marriages. Look on the walls of people's homes, and you see framed shots of their kids' high school or college graduations, but certainly no photos of the thousands of forgettable hours these kids spent in classrooms. Similarly, hunters photograph our moments of triumph, not the long stretches of time between, when we fail—perhaps for weeks at a time—to even see a buck.

Opponents of hunting call these kinds of photos "horn porn," seeing them as crass moments of celebratory male bonding around the violent subjugation of nature. While I share some of this critique of men and hunting, I also know that there are deeper layers of meaning in these photos, beyond simply seeing them as pornographic money shots. In *Picturing Men,* one of my favorite books, John Ibson examines the changing ways that men pose together for photographs. In the early decades of the twentieth century, men routinely posed draped all over each other—holding hands, arm in arm, hugging, cheek-to-cheek, sitting on each other's laps. Men displayed comfort and what now seems a playful innocence with physical closeness. By the mid-twentieth century—with the exception of a blip during World War II, when soldiers again frequently posed with playful physical intimacy—the unspoken conventions of men posing for studio portraits or informal snapshots changed. Perhaps in response to a rise in homophobia in the culture, men now distanced themselves from each other, less often hugging or touching each other. In later twentieth century photos, the spaces between men's bodies are often mediated by objects—sports equipment, guns, dead animals.

I now look again at the photo of "Mike's First Buck." Neither Dad, Gramps nor I are touching each other. The dead buck lies between, mediating the space that otherwise separates us. I grip the left side of the buck's antler; Dad completes the symmetry by holding up the right. It demeans the deeper meanings of this photo to see it simply as a moment of "male bonding." This is a photo of intimacy, but one that reveals the cultural constraints on men's expressions of love for each other. When direct avenues of experiencing intimacy are blocked—as they routinely are for boys and men—we sometimes find other, perhaps distorted ways that involve violence and domination to establish moments of meaningful connection with others.

My Dad was warm and loving, but like so many fathers in the 1950's, he was absent much of the time during my early childhood: working at the high school, traveling to basketball games, off on hunting trips, away for weekends or summer tours with the Naval Reserve. Mom was constantly there for my sisters and me, day-to-day and moment-to-moment: delivering three meals a day; caring for us when we were sick; walking us to school; reading a book together, curled up on the couch after school. This routine intertwining of mothers' daily lives with those of their children, coupled with the separation of fathers, makes kids' rare moments with Dad—for me, a weekend deer hunt, our annual trip to San Francisco for a Giants' game, or a game of catch in the yard—lodge in the memory with an emotional salience far more profound than its apparent surface meaning.

The constraints on expressions of physical intimacy between men run deep. When I was very young, after Mom bathed, dressed and tucked me in to bed, Dad would step into my room. I would fold my hands, shut my eyes and say my "now I lay me down to sleep" prayer. Dad would say "good night Pal," kiss me, and leave my door open a crack, a shaft of hallway light cutting across my dark bedroom.

Once, when I was about twelve, Dad said, "Mike, I like kissing you good night, but if you are ever uncomfortable with it, just tell me."

I said, "It's okay."

But not too long after, when Dad leaned over to kiss me one night, I spontaneously turned my face away from him. He pulled back, said good night and left my room. I don't remember having decided in advance that

King of the Wild Suburb

Joe stood sentry over my sleeping head for years (circa 1958).

I didn't want Dad kissing me anymore, but I turned away from him in that moment, and he read my rejection. I'd not kiss Dad again until the morning of his brain surgery, more than a decade later.

○

During the few weeks following my big kill, we awaited the return of the stuffed buck from the taxidermist. In preparation, Dad moved Joe, the mounted buck who had towered over my sleeping head for as long as I could remember, from my bedroom to the family dining room. When my buck arrived, we dubbed him Sam, and hung him directly over my bed where Joe had been. Sam was mounted in a "sneak" pose, head down, antlers laid back, in the posture he'd struck the moment we'd first seen him crashing through the brush. Alone in my bedroom that first night, I looked into Sam's glass eyes. My tears welled up; determined, I fought them back. In that moment I told myself—and pledged in a whisper to this buck—that I would never, ever shoot another deer.

This remained a secret between Sam and me. I continued to hunt with Dad and Gramps for the next couple of years. The one last time I had a clear shot at a buck, I purposely pulled back on my aim, exploding the dirt behind his back feet. The buck danced and skipped through the brush, over a ridge to safety.

Dad asked me how I could have missed such a close shot, "A bit of buck fever?"

I avoided Dad's eyes.

"I don't know," I said, "I thought I was right on him."

I held up my rifle in the palms of both hands and scrutinized it, as a Little Leaguer will inspect the webbing of his mitt after muffing a routine ground ball.

8
Heroic Noses

"Please, Daddy, smash your nose! Smash it flat for us!"

Dad leaned back in his chair and chuckled. The Messner family was nearly done with dinner, four of us still sitting at the oval Formica table, Mom standing at the stove, scraping up a final scoop of mashed potatoes to offer to anybody who was still hungry.

"No, Russ, don't you dare! I hate it when you do that," she said, suppressing the smile that would betray her part in this drama.

"Yes-yes, *please*," Linny begged.

Terry added, "I'll rub your back if you do, Daddy, please?"

To a three-kid chorus of "YAY" and mom's discordant "Oh, *no*," Dad pressed down on his nose with his index and middle fingers, removed his hand, and revealed a nose flattened to his face. As the cheering subsided, he re-shaped his nose with both hands, and giggled with the rest of us.

Dad said he couldn't even remember how many times he'd broken his nose playing football. It's no wonder, when you considered that the helmets they wore in those days were soft padded leather, with no face-guard. He was lucky he had teeth.

Dad's nose, malleable as Gumby, was the opposite of Gramps' bony red, scythe-like nose. Once when I was little, sitting next to Gramps at his desk, I reached out, and with the tip of my uninvited index finger, traced the long curving arc from the bridge to the end of his nose.

He just laughed: "Broke it twice, my boy. Once, I ran into a ladder. The other time, into a fist."

As a result, Gramps couldn't breathe clearly out of the left nostril, so as he sat reading the paper after dinner, he'd stick his left index finger into the space between his nose and cheekbone, pulling open a passage for air. Over the years, this created a permanent dent next to Gramps' bony nose.

By contrast, my nose is, well, normal. I took a basketball or two in the nose in my day but never broke it. Never played tackle football. In fifth grade, in a touch football game, husky crew-cutted Mark Leffler ran directly at me, and I held my ground to tag him, waiting for his feint to the left or the right to avoid me; instead, he ran right through me. Mr. McQuiddy blew his whistle and stood directly above me as I lay flat on my back in the damp grass.

"Well, you tagged him, Mike."

Yeah, I'd tagged him down, but the vibrations in my fillings from that hit decided for me right then and there that football was not for me. So I played basketball—a contact sport, not a collision sport.

Unlike Gramps, I never got into a real fistfight in my life. Guys who got in fights, I reasoned, were stupid. My only opportunity to get into a real fight came in junior high, and I just plain ran away, which left me feeling simultaneously clever and cowardly. My shame was a private wound, exposed by the widening chasm between my private fantasies of fearless heroism and my real-life avoidance of anything physically violent or even excessively rough.

Starting in the second grade, as Mrs. Tatum droned on about penmanship or spelling, I conjured a recurring heroic fantasy. An armed bad guy suddenly enters our placid classroom, taking us all hostage. Through cleverness, brave and efficient use of violence, and my mastery of guns, I disarm the evil villain and save my classmates. In subsequent iterations of this fantasy, the gunman threatens specific girls. From third through sixth grade, I was madly in love with Nancy Masters, a cute auburn-haired girl with pink tear-drop-framed glasses. During those grade school years, unbeknownst to Nancy, I must have saved her from hundreds of imaginary thugs and criminals. If something like this ever really happened, I told myself, I would be the brave one who puts his life on the line and saves everybody. And the girls—Nancy in particular—would admire me ever so much more than all the other boys who would sit saucer-eyed, frozen with fear at their desks. In such fantasies, I was always the hero. But my tendency in real life to run like a scared chicken from fights made me wonder: would I really be brave, if push came to shove?

I never fought in a war, either. As an eighteen-year-old, I'd lucked out in avoiding the draft. A year later, at Chico State University, I read Marx, Sartre, and de Beauvoir. I grew my hair long, announced I was against the war, despised patriarchy, and hated organized sports—especially football. I joined the co-ed badminton team, and the rest of the time pretty much just sat around reading, when I wasn't partying with my friends. All of this kept my nose in pretty much pristine condition (if not always entirely clean).

Make love, not war, I chanted with my generation. And I might well have added: swat shuttlecocks, not linebackers; throw peace signs, not fists; lift roach clips, not ladders. I was a gentle "new" man, I told myself—against war, guns, football, and all forms of violence. But something inside me still craved some form of heroic distinction, something different—opposed, even—to my father's heroism.

○

Dad and I walked out of the sweltering heat of a Chico summer day into the refrigerated air of Raley's Grocery Store. It was 1974. Dad was visiting me at my college pad for a couple days, and after taking one look at my paltry pantry, he offered to take me to the grocery store to stock up on food. As I wheeled the grocery cart past the frozen foods section, I stopped abruptly to avoid a head-on collision with my professor, Larry Wenzel. At six-foot-four, with a full shock of gray hair and a bristly walrus mustache, Larry cut quite a figure, whether in the classroom or at the grocery store.

"Hi there!" Larry said with a smile.

My hands clenched the push-handle of the grocery basket as I stood between Dad and Larry. There were sudden explosions in my mind, as though I was ducking for cover in no-man's land between opposing artillery fire.

I barely managed, "Oh, hi Larry."

"How's your summer going?" he asked.

"Good, good."

There was a pause, as though the artillery fire had ceased in anticipation of truce talks. Dad stood to my left wearing a polo shirt, hands in the pockets of his Bermuda shorts, his black coaching shoes topped by white tube-socks pulled halfway up his thick calves. He might as well have been wearing a whistle and carrying a clipboard. Larry wore brown khaki pants, light boots and the blue button-down cotton work shirt that was *de rigueur* for campus revolutionaries. He looked at me expectantly, gave a little laugh as though he had seen this scene a million times—some newly radicalized kid trying to squirm away from what feels suddenly like an irreconcilable contradiction, tearing him in two.

"Uh, well, good to see you Larry," I said as I wheeled the cart toward the checkout.

As Dad and I loaded the groceries into the car he asked, "So, that was one of your professors?"

"Oh, yeah," I said, "Larry Wenzel. He was a Minor League Baseball player and was in the Marines during the war."

I immediately felt like a heel for not introducing Larry and Dad. And it's funny to think today about how much they had in common—the same age, former athletes, World War II veterans. But to me, they represented two parts of myself that I could not then reconcile—Dad was the past, the false part of me that I had rejected; Larry was the future, the new, the emergent real me.

I met Larry Wenzel when I took his sociological theory class during my first semester at Chico State. It was the Fall of 1972. I was twenty years old, unsure of myself and just awakening to the radical ruptures of culture and politics taking place around me. Larry Wenzel seemed to be everything that I could hope to become: intellectual, politically radical, and funny as hell. Early in that semester, I was sitting with the other students in the class, awaiting the arrival of Professor Wenzel. Already, I was in awe of him. Usually he'd just come in, sit down on a table in front of the classroom, start talking, and we would listen in fascination as he discussed the major traditions and concepts of sociological theory, weaving them together with his vast knowledge of philosophy and current events. Emile Durkheim, Max Weber and Karl Marx (mostly Marx, to be sure) came alive as Larry discussed current labor struggles in the U.S., the Vietnam War, or social movements in Latin America. On this day, he entered the classroom without a word, and uncharacteristically began to write on the chalkboard.

"To do is to be."—Descartes

It immediately became clear that Larry was about to deliver some profound lesson on the philosophical roots of modern social theory, so we all began dutifully reproducing this wisdom in our notes, as he continued to write.

"To be is to do."—Sartre

He glanced over his shoulder at us, and with a twinkle in his eye said, "I hope you're getting this," and wrote:

"Do-be-do-be-do."—*Sinatra*

Larry made bold predictions from the bully pulpit of his classroom. During the mid-70's energy crisis, he proclaimed that he planned to live long enough to see the nation run out of gasoline. The roomful of young college students tittered as Larry declared, "I picture myself one day setting up my lawn chair right next to Interstate 5, sitting down with a pitcher of iced lemonade, and watching them tear up that useless highway."

He also openly speculated about when—not *if*—we'd experience socialism in our lifetimes.

My unforgettable Larry Wenzel moment came in September 1973, in his class entitled "Social Change." At the beginning of the semester, he noted that the Cold War had created the illusion that history had stopped in two inhumane dead ends: Corporate capitalism, and Stalinism. However, he said, there was a fascinating experiment currently taking place in Chile, where the people had democratically elected a socialist president, Salvador Allende. Larry saw this as a historic "third road," that created room for optimism that a society could move democratically and peacefully toward equality and justice. We would study Chile this semester, he told us, and treat it as a living laboratory of social change. A week later, a Nixon-Kissinger-CIA-backed military coup overthrew and murdered Allende, ended Chilean democracy and instituted a reign of violent terror that would last years. The day after the coup, Professor Wenzel walked into the classroom, red-faced and visibly shaken. He held up his fist in the familiar "power" salute, and said to us, "Do you know what this means?"

Pens in hand, we silently waited to hear the answer that we would write into our notes. He opened his hand, palm facing us, and one-by-one began to close each finger, starting with the little finger, "This is the environmental movement; this is the women's movement; this is the civil rights movement; this is the anti-war movement; and this," pausing briefly as he closed his thumb, "this is the labor movement."

Now, once again holding up his closed fist, he pounded it into his other hand, "Together, they can SMASH *capitalism!*"

And then he walked out of the classroom; lesson delivered for the day.

Over my four years in Chico, I occasionally went to Larry's house, drank beer with him and smoked a joint. Books lined the walls of his living room, from floor to ceiling. He told me about his younger Mexican girlfriend who lived nearby. They would sit in the living room late into the night, he said, drinking red wine and reading aloud from the Chilean poet Pablo Neruda.

Michael A. Messner

What was not to admire about this radical man? How could I ever go back to respecting my father's outmoded style of masculinity?

Over time, fissures appeared in the romantic edifice of Larry Wenzel. His social change class had been given a take-home final exam on how best to make a revolution in the U.S. One small group of students, he told me, had decided to arm themselves with screwdrivers and simply dismantle everything around them, starting with the restrooms at Chico State University. Larry thought it brilliant and hilariously subversive to imagine that a secret collective could dismantle the capitalist war machine, one screw at a time.

I reveled in the revolutionary zeal of this idea too, until I told my friend Walter Irish about it. Walter was a rebel poet with whom I'd lived in a trailer-home during our first year at college. I'd met him two years earlier in Salinas, when we'd both worked as summer YMCA day camp counselors. That summer, the bus dropped us daily in a semi-wild place called Pine Canyon. As I tried in vain to get a dozen ten-year-old boys to participate in structured activities like weaving lanyards, Walter took his kids for hours-long hikes, stopping to let them play in muddy creek bottoms, and then ending up on the tops of mountains, where he and his kids would yell in unison—*FUUUUCK!*—and then howl in glee as their voices bounced around Pine Canyon. The kids loved Walter, dubbed him Uncle Waldo, and the name stuck. I admired Uncle Waldo, too. Three years my senior, he put radical books into my hands and told me to read them: Jack Kerouac's *On the Road*, *The Autobiography of Malcolm X*, Richard Brautigan's *A Confederate General from Big Sur,* and of course Allen Ginsberg's *Howl*. Walter admired rebellious freethinking and was suspicious of all orthodoxy, be it right, left, or religious. When I told him about the secret revolutionary dismantling of the restrooms, I expected him to share my glee. But he didn't. Instead, he read this idea through his own working class background, and his response was immediate and from his gut, "That's stupid. All that will do is create work for maintenance men. What kind of Marxist tries to make a revolution by alienating working class people?"

I knew immediately that Uncle Waldo was right. Heck, even if we could have gotten into the Pentagon and dismantled every single toilet stall, it wouldn't have slowed the war machine a whit—but *University* restrooms? The main appeal of this sort of idea, I realized, was how it fulfilled an adolescent desire to make a dramatic screw-you gesture to the adult world. That made me wonder: why did Larry Wenzel think this was such a delicious idea?

Larry's major fall from grace, for me, was the day he revealed his old school sexism. During my last semester at Chico State, as I was completing my master's degree, I was employed to teach my own introductory sociology class. I was extremely proud and saw this as the first concrete sign that I might actually become a professor, just like Larry.

When I told Larry the good news, he winked at me and said, "Well, be sure to get all you can."

I thought he was talking about the paltry pay, and I said "I don't think there's any room for negotiation with the salary."

He laughed. "No! I'm talking about the girls! You won't believe it, Mike. Get all you can!"

I was repelled. What Larry had said to me was precisely the stuff I'd been reading about in the nascent Women's Liberation literature. Women had separated from the anti-war movement to form a feminist movement partly because men of the "new" left had treated them like dirt. These very men who positioned themselves as leaders of a revolution that would bring about peace, equality and freedom for all were treating women within their movement as props, personal assistants, and sexual objects of conquest. Suddenly I could see that in having switched my desire for a heroic role model from conservative Dad to radical Larry, I had simply switched my focus to a new and differently flawed form of *male* heroism.

Dad was no feminist. He too was old-school, but in the style of the gentleman who is faithful to his wife and sees women as deserving their husbands' protection and fidelity. The post-war middle class ideal of separate gendered worlds that my parents had lived by—Dad the breadwinner, Mom in the domestic realm—was what the feminist women around me were fighting to change. Though disenchanted with Larry's leftist sexism, I had no desire to return to Dad's chivalrous masculinity either. Still, I realized that Dad's treatment of women expressed a consistent integrity I could respect. By contrast, I could neither follow nor respect Larry's. I continued to feel an appreciative affection toward Larry Wenzel, and kept in touch with him until his death in 2002. But by the time I'd left Chico for my first teaching job in 1976, I no longer viewed him as a role model for my future. Instead, I'd begun to look more to women for progressive ideas and values, and to find other men in my life who shared my emergent feminist ideals.

Many times over the years I have been asked by students or by someone who has read one of my books how or why I became a feminist. I have never came up with a profound answer to this question. Most of the men of my generation who came to identify with feminism tell stories of grief, abuse or masculine failure—having been put down by other kids or by one's father for being a sissy; always getting picked last when sports teams were chosen; having to endure seeing one's mother or sister sexually abused or raped. I don't have any of these kinds of stories in my past. Instead, I usually chalk it up to context and history: I was in college right when the women's movement was taking off, my women friends were in consciousness raising groups, and began to challenge men on our sexism. However, people have pointed out to me that most men of my generation weren't affected by that context in the same way I was. They asked, "What was it about *you?*" This question pushes me to consider my longstanding desire to be accepted and approved of by women—initially by my mother and my two sisters. Linny and Terry used to kid me that they influenced my identification with women. When Dad was away for Naval Reserve tours, my sisters would smear red rouge on my cheeks and gleefully dress me up in girls' clothes—a wig on my head, my hands in a rabbit-fur muff, high-heeled shoes—like I was their little doll.

"Oh, God," Mom would laugh, "Daddy would just die to see his son like this!"

With all due respect to the rabbit-muff theory, I think my initial opening to feminism was grounded in my early aversions to fighting, war, hunting and football. Initially, these were not intellectual or political positions; they were gut-level feelings of fear and loathing. My philosophical analysis of why I rejected these things came later, and I laid this analysis atop my ambivalence like a shiny façade on a porous and creaky structure. The underlying feelings of fear and loathing had brought confusion and private shame. The analysis—I am anti-war, anti-violence, pro-feminist because it is good and noble to be so—brought pride, and enabled me to take public positions against the things I abhorred. So, in a way, feminism and the other 1970's progressive movements that I attached myself to offered me a convenient way to rationalize feelings I already had, but those I'd not been able to own with pride.

Over the years, the sociologist in me has wanted to see my anti-violence beliefs and my feminist teaching and writing as grounded in an ethical choice to commit myself to the goals of the progressive social movements of my time. I realize now that there was more to it than that—I suspect there was an elective affinity between the values of these movements and the inchoate feelings I already had—that getting blasted in the face with a fist or crushed by another guy's body sucked; that being in a war was not for me. Now given form by feminism and anti-war movements, these feelings seemed to have a higher meaning and purpose. However, this crystallization of my progressive world view and these antipathies coexisted in an uneasy tension with my continued fantasies of male heroism in these very realms. I retained a private fascination and a quiet reverence for Dad's and Gramps' heroics in wars, industrial strikes, fistfights, and the gridiron.

When I was a kid, I thought that Gramps' and Dad's noses told heroic, manly stories, and that my nose told no story at all. I now see that it does. My intact nose is the beneficiary of my choices to run away from fights, to avoid violent sports, and to escape from warfare. If I'd been a poor, working class kid like Gramps, I'd likely have had little choice but to duke it out with young ruffians, and could easily have ended up drafted into the Army as a foot soldier. If I'd been an upwardly-mobile kid from a working class family like Dad, I may have had greater affinity for a game like football, as a way to battle my way into college. And I could easily have been drawn during college into NROTC, where I might have become a Naval officer. But my nose tells a different story. Mine is a nose unmarked by the fact of privilege—privilege made possible by the foundation that Gramps and Dad built, and set me upon.

9
La Brea Tar Pits

"I can't handle driving down Main Street," I said.

Earlier, Linny had phoned in tears to tell us that the flag at the high school was flying at half-mast. I just didn't think I could look at it. When Dad came to Salinas in 1947, a freshly-minted coach from U.C. Berkeley and the U.S. Navy, Salinas High School was known simply as The High School, the beloved Spanish-style Main Street centerpiece. Thirty years later, we still called it The High School, despite the fact that the growing town had added two more public high schools and a private Catholic one.

On this morning, a day after Dad's death in 1977, we drove to the mortuary to "make arrangements." Mom said she wanted to see the flag, so I reluctantly drove us down Main Street. The flag was indeed at half-mast, barely fluttering in the warmth of September's Indian Summer. My eyes welled up, but I fought my tears back.

My feelings were deflected by Mom's observation: "Look. Everybody's going about their business. Don't they know?"

Indeed, cars honked and rolled on Main Street. High school kids strolled casually across the green lawn directly beneath the drooping flag, cradling books, laughing to each other, apparently oblivious to the momentous import of this day when the world stopped for my family.

○

"Dad was a flash," Linny has often said, "but never in a braggy sort of way."

My sister is right. Our father was a big-shot. But he would never go out of his way to tell you about his accomplishments, preferring his actions to do the talking. When I was a boy, I wanted to be a big-shot athlete, just like Dad. I shot baskets, incessantly, on our driveway. I kept track of my makes and misses from key spots, as though I could quantify my rise to greatness. During my seventh-grade Thanksgiving and Christmas vacations, I kept a written log of the number of minutes I spent on the driveway, perfecting my shot. I hoped to specialize in long-distance shooting, like Rusty Critchfield, the sharpshooting star on Dad's Salinas High team from 1961 to 1963.

One day, Dad came out on the driveway, stood under the basket and started feeding passes to me as I darted around the court, swishing shot after shot. I kept waiting for him to say something like "wow," or "great shot," but he just kept silently feeding me bounce passes.

When I couldn't take it any more I said, "I'm getting to be a pretty good shot."

Dad held the ball for a moment before throwing it back.

"When you're a good shot, people will say you are a good shot. You don't have to point it out."

Clunk went my next shot off the back iron.

A year before Dad died, I'd completed my master's degree in sociology. On a rare trip home to Salinas, I sipped a beer in the backyard as Dad poked a chicken leg on his smoking barbeque. I ribbed Dad that I now held a higher degree than his mere bachelor's.

"Well," he said, referring to his rank as U.S. Navy Captain, "I don't see four bars on your shoulders."

Dad wouldn't go out of his way to lord his accomplishments over anybody, but I guess when his son tried to pull rank on him, he wasn't above putting me back in my place. "No brag, just fact," the geriatric cowboy actor Walter Brennan would say in his 1967 TV show *The Guns of Will Sonnett*, and this seemed to express a version of Dad's philosophy of how to be a big-shot. Be good at what you do, be a standout, but don't brag, don't (as we would say today) self-promote.

Which is not to say that Dad wasn't competitive. When he played against us kids—whether it was basketball, badminton or checkers—he made it clear that he would never let us win: "That way, when you finally beat me, you'll know you earned it."

The first time I beat Dad one-on-one in basketball, I was eleven years old. It shouldn't really have happened. My victory was a stroke of luck that Dad immediately trumped with a miracle. Dad had taken me over to the high school gym, as he occasionally would on a Saturday. He'd open the door with his keys, and the entire cavernous building—locker room, showers, and cracker box gym—would be ours. As I inhaled the musty odors of the locker room, I was certain that I was the luckiest boy in Salinas.

Dad and I would dress in the coaches' dressing room, and I'd always get out to the court before him. The first slaps of the ball on the varnished wood floor of the empty gym ricocheted off the walls and the metal girders above me. The floor groaned under my feet as I carefully laid in my first shot. (My friend Donnie and I had agreed that it was cosmically important always to make your first shot of the day.) Dad strolled on to the court in his gray sweats, did some jumping jacks to loosen up, took a few shots, and then gave me first outs.

I was young, still considerably shorter than Dad, but he'd let the score stay close to keep it interesting, until finishing me off at the end. But on this day, with the score tied at game point, for some reason his winning shot bounced awry. I chased down the long rebound and had just enough room to launch an eighteen-footer from the right side of the key as Dad rushed at me, yelling like a banshee, arms wind-milling. The ball left my fingertips, floated like a feather over Dad's outstretched hands, swished through net, fell to the floor and bounced up toward the free throw line. Vanquished, Dad reflexively grabbed the ball, and with a terrible roar hurled it sidearm the full length of the court. The ball sailed like a missile, slapped the backboard and banked neatly into the basket. Dad looked at me, smiled and shrugged as though he made seventy-foot shots every day. I stood in slack-jawed awe. A full two years would pass before I'd beat Dad again.

Dad was always a winner. Before the war, he'd played football for U.C. Berkeley—*Cal* was what he called it. If you asked him what position he played, he'd answer with mock self-aggrandizement, "*Position?* We didn't play *positions* in my day; we played *football*."

He went both ways: defensive back and offensive fullback. And he was the punter. On the rare occasion that he'd talk about his football career, he'd say that his one regret was that a broken arm sidelined him for most of his senior season. The day after he broke his arm, the October 7, 1942 sports page of the *San Francisco Examiner* ran a banner headline, "Messner,

Bear Back, Breaks Arm." That same day, *San Francisco Chronicle* sports editor Bill Leiser ran a column with the headline, "Bears Lose Messner, Only Remaining Man Who Can Really Kick," and noted in the article, "The loss is quite definite. His forearm is busted cleanly."

After the war, Dad finished his teaching credential at Cal, and moved with Mom and newborn Terry to Salinas. There Dad served the next ten years as the football coach, and a quarter century as the varsity basketball coach at the high school. Over the years, he won plenty of championships and coach-of-the-year awards. But—following his Cal coach Stub Allison—he adhered to a philosophy that winning is of secondary importance. A coach's primary goal is to be a teacher who helps to shape young men into good citizens.

Once a week, Dad would stop basketball practice ten minutes early, and tell his sweaty charges to sit on the floor in the middle of the gym. There he would stand and deliver one of his speeches about "life." When I was on Dad's team during my junior and senior years, I found these moments excruciating. Tortured, I'd pick at the rubber on my shoe, avoiding eye contact with anybody. Apparently oblivious to my pain, Dad would deliver lessons about honesty, hard work, responsibility, and making sacrifices for your teammates. He'd tell us that how we played the game of basketball was preparation for the kinds of men we were going to be later, in our families and our jobs.

"Sports is life," he would routinely summarize.

Invariably, at the end of every speech, he would give us the same practical advice before sending us off to the showers:

"Fellas, the evenings are getting colder, so be sure to dry your heads good before you go outside."

Twenty years after his death, Dad was one of the first inductees into the Salinas High School Sports Hall of Fame. I made a short speech at the ceremony, accepting the award on behalf of my family. I joked that my own athletic mediocrity ensured that this would be the only such acceptance speech I'd ever make. I drew from the research I'd done with former athletes, and said that the most important positive memories people tend to have about their coaches are usually not from games, they are from practices. And when I told the stories of Dad's speeches, and recalled his advice to dry our heads, I could see a smattering of his former players in the audience—some older than me, some younger—smiling and nodding in recognition. I had no trouble now making eye contact with these men.

Dad coached football at the high school for ten years, and basketball for a quarter-century.

○

"Russ Messner, Salinas' 'Mr. Basketball' Dies" read the headline of the September 29, 1977 *Salinas Californian*. Dad had died the previous day at Stanford Hospital in Palo Alto. The morning Dad died I was busy moving to a small house in Sacramento with my girlfriend Judith. Just a bit after noon, the phone rang as I was heading out the door of my now-vacant apartment, cradling the last carton of kitchen utensils. Mom was crying.

"Mike honey, I think Daddy's died."

He was still on a respirator, she told me, but he was gone. He'd been working hard, doing physical therapy that morning at the hospital, Mom at his side, when suddenly he gasped, convulsed for a few moments, and despite immediate CPR, died. Judith drove me to Palo Alto to the hospital, and later that day to Salinas.

The previous January, Dad had been diagnosed with colon cancer. I didn't bother going to Salinas for the surgery. It was routine, he told us all. "Dad's a rock," we told each other. He came out of it brimming with apparent optimism.

"They say they got it all," he told us.

He didn't have chemo or radiation therapy. Instead, on the advice of Dr. Nunes, he took Mom on a vacation to Hawaii. By August, Dad started having trouble with his coordination; the cancer had reappeared in his brain. He was fifty-six years old.

"It's just a little spot on the surface of my brain," I heard him reassuring Gramps on the phone, "The doc will take it off and I'll be fine."

I went to Salinas for this one. I visited Dad as he lay in his bed the morning of the surgery. I didn't know what to say. As I left him, I kissed the top of his balding head.

I sat for hours with Mom and Terry in the waiting room. As we waited, I tried to read a book entitled *The Dialectical Imagination*, dutifully underlining indecipherable passages like "Sartre severed subjectivity from objectivity in a way that denied reconciliation even as a utopian possibility." When the surgeon finally came out, he spoke to us on the fly, barely stopping to say that he had nothing definitive to tell us about the surgery on Dad's head. Terry, utilizing her skills as the family combatant, cornered him as he tried to walk away and demanded he tell us exactly what was going on. He stopped long enough to say simply and emphatically, "We—just—don't—know."

What we did know, soon after the surgery, was that Dad's wires were cut. Lying in his hospital bed, severely aphasic, Dad was frustrated with his inability to express himself. When he wanted to say something, his brain sabotaged his efforts. In frustration, he would grimace and blurt out the words "La Brea Tar Pits." We had visited the La Brea Tar Pits many years earlier, during one of our family vacations to Disneyland. I'd been transfixed by the small lake—right in the middle of Los Angeles—still bubbling its ancient tar and noxious methane fumes. A model of a huge-tusked mammoth struggles, hopelessly mired in the middle of the tar-filled lake, as a smaller adult, presumably a female, and a tiny baby toe up to the water's edge, watching, helpless. We had no clue why Dad's brain now transmitted "La Brea Tar Pits" to his lips. Maybe, I assumed at the time, the brain surgery had left that one synapse open for words, like a spillway that diverts water from a dammed lake. But I now wonder if Dad was conveying to us as best he could that he felt stuck, unable to move or to express his thoughts, as his wife, children and friends toed up to his hospital bed, watching, talking, hoping, but apparently unable to pull him out of the muck. In the days that followed, in moments of frustrated dark humor, my family would shrug and repeat, "La Brea Tar Pits."

We moved Dad to Stanford hospital a week later, in the hopes that their doctors would know more. We drove in caravan—Dad and Mom with their dear friends Margaret and Jack Stirling, my sisters and I following in my car. We took a roundabout route leaving Salinas, because Mom wanted to drive by 801 Bautista Drive, pointing out our house to Dad through the car window, for what turned out to be one last time.

Dad had one more brain surgery at Stanford, from which he emerged further debilitated. The last time I walked into the hospital room, Dad greeted me with a half-smile and a sweet "Oh," of recognition. I could not stay long. Really, I would not stay long, could not endure the horror of seeing Dad, his head turbaned with bandages, his voice nearly gone, half his body paralyzed. Mom bravely endured, spending every waking minute by Dad's side, talking with him, touching him, singing to buoy his spirits and hers. I left: I drove ten miles up Highway 101 to San Mateo, seeking solace at my childhood friend Donnie Hallstone's apartment. That evening, we fired up a bong. I stared into the cloud of smoke I had exhaled into the middle of the living room and murmured, "La Brea Tar Pits."

My inability to confront the horror of Dad's condition was more than mere squeamishness. In recent years, I'd grown distant from Dad. I didn't visit often. I'd grown and changed, I told myself, and was now different from Dad—intellectual, politically progressive. I'd stopped going hunting with him. And I was at the height of my condemnation of the evils of sports. Once when I was visiting home, Dad told me about two young guys he'd met in Tahoe, realtors who were helping him buy an investment property. When he said in admiration, "they're both *real jocks,*" I believe I may have smirked. Another time, standing with Dad in front of his smoking barbeque, I mentioned that I was planning to go from Salinas "down to Oakland."

He said, "That would be *up* to Oakland, since it's north."

"That's arbitrary," I replied.

"What are you talking about?" he asked.

"Look," I said, falling into my I-have-a-Masters-degree-in-sociology mode, "The first world map makers were European imperialists. They insisted on mapping Europe as the center of the universe, on top of everybody else. That's why we think of north as 'up'."

Dad rolled his eyeballs, "That's the stupidest thing I've ever heard."

Trying to control my rage at his ignorance, I introduced a visual example. "Look, you could take a globe in your hands, and tip it upside down, and now South would be up."

"Yeah," he replied with a dismissive laugh, "and then everybody would fall off."

For months, I repeated this story to all of my friends, to illustrate the hopeless intellectual chasm that had opened between my father and me.

○

These days, when I think of Dad, I always think of good things. He is an occasional but reassuring presence in my dreams—usually it's a basketball game, and he's yelling instructions to me from the sidelines. There was nothing in Dad's life that makes me feel angry, hurt, or resentful (I even forgive him for voting for Nixon). But it still rankles that he kept the severity of his cancer from us. I'm now certain that after his colon cancer surgery, his doctor told him he was terminal—why otherwise would he have dispatched Dad to Hawaii instead of to chemotherapy? Dad decided to "protect" Mom, his kids and his parents from this terrible truth by telling us that it was not so bad, that he was going to be okay. He wasn't okay. The autopsy, performed the day after he died, said that Dad died from a "massive pulmonary embolism," a large blood clot that likely broke loose during his physical therapy, lodging in his heart and lungs. It also revealed that Dad had cancer of the everything: "Resected carcinoma of the colon…metastases to lymph nodes, peritoneal cavity, lung, adrenal gland and liver."

I've read the grim autopsy report. But for years, I have claimed in lectures and in my writings about men's health that masculinity killed my father. Within a few short months, cancer quickly dropped the man who, to our family, had always seemed like the Rock of Gibraltar. And that, I think, was the root of the problem. Dad was a big-shot, a public success. But lofty public status comes with a price tag: too often, men pay with poor health, shorter lives, emotionally shallow relationships, and less time spent with loved ones. Currently, American women are expected to live about five years longer than men. Most of this gap is not due to nature but to men's adherence to narrow and dangerous conceptions of masculinity. Men tend to smoke and drink more than women; we engage in violence and high-risk behavior at much higher rates than women do; we tend to be slower than women to ask for professional medical help; and we are taught to downplay or ignore our own pain.

Dad didn't smoke. He drank moderately and was not violent. He was careful and deliberate behind the wheel of a car. But as a star football player and as a wartime naval officer, he had been taught that a real man ignores pain and pays whatever price is necessary to support his team or country. His conservative Lutheranism buttressed this lesson—that a man's first responsibility was as a family breadwinner who worked hard and sacrificed himself, day in and day out, for the good of his family. Dad was proud that he'd never let a head cold or a sore back keep him from going to work. He "played through the pain," kept his complaints to himself, and never revealed his own discomfort or fears. When he started having troubles with his bowels, he ignored it and started to use more laxatives.

Shortly after his colon surgery, Dad told me with an uncharacteristic tinge of embarrassment that when he first spotted a bit of blood in his stool, "I thought it was a piece of tomato, I don't know."

He'd finally gone to the doctor when he couldn't stand it any longer, and by then it was too late. He died with nearly a year's worth of accumulated "sick leave" at the high school.

○

Back home with Mom on the evening of Dad's death, I said to Gramps on the phone, "I wish I could be there with you and Granny."

Gramps' voice was thin and clear: "Nope, you done right. You should be there with your mom."

Three weeks later, I was back in Salinas. Dad hadn't written out his wishes for burial or cremation. Only 56, perhaps he hadn't really thought these things through. Mom said he'd wanted to be cremated, but we had no clue what to do with his remains. He wasn't enough of a career Navy guy to have wanted his ashes scattered at sea, and it didn't seem likely we could bury his ashes under the Salinas High gym, or Cal's Memorial Stadium. One of us, I don't remember who, thought of Chualar Canyon. A day after spreading Dad's ashes, I tried to chronicle my feelings in a poem.

October, 1977

This crisp sunny October day
reminds me of deer hunting days long past

But today I'm in a small plane with my sisters
and Charlie, an old hunting companion of my father's,
is the pilot

As we fly and talk about landmarks and weather
my thoughts are focused
on the heavy paper bag I hold firmly
with both hands on my lap

Somehow I'd expected a more dignified container
for my father's ashes, but it doesn't matter

My fingers press into the bag as though
I can get just one more reassuring touch—
just one more caress from this man

But my hands sense only cold dryness—
I shiver as my hands feel the coarseness
of the bag's contents
(he's not really here—this is only symbolic)

There's the old "Olive Trees" area we used to hunt
(I was small and the climb was steep—
I'd grab his belt and he'd haul me up the hill—
could anyone be stronger than he?)

And there's the little green cabin:
Here my father and grandfather taught me
cooking, dirty jokes, farting, togetherness,
manhood

Ah, and there it is:
near the top-country—the Esterbrook Flats—
tucked between the steep brush-covered mountains,
a serene meadow
sparsely covered with strong oaks

Here is where the cattle and the deer come
to rest and water—indeed, this is here we used to rest
and drink from our canteens after a long morning hunt

A natural resting place

Charlie slows the plane
at low altitude over the Flats—
I can see my arm extending the bag out the window
(I only hesitate a moment)
the gray ashes release into the wind

We hardly speak or look back as we fly
back up the Salinas Valley
my hands tremble as I drop the empty bag to the floor

I hurt, but he feels no pain now…
for me, it is just the first step
in letting go of my father

Michael A. Messner

Dad and I in Chualar Canyon (circa 1960).

I xeroxed the single typewritten page and presented it to my family members in laminated plastic. A few days later, I drove to Oakland to see Granny and Gramps. After dinner, I sat with Gramps at the dining room table and gave him the poem. He read it slowly, seeming to savor the words. He glanced up at me from under his red visor, tears coursing down his lined face.

"That's just fine," he sobbed, "When I go, I want you to do the same for me."

Gramps dabbed his cheek with a napkin and said in a near whisper, "You know, when I'd go to Salinas, I'd walk across the street with your dad, and people would wave and say hello. Everybody knew him. I admired him so much."

In this moment, Dad towered like Mount Rushmore over the two of us.

"Me too," I said, "Me too."

10
Tall Tales

The rattlesnake stared straight up the barrel of my rifle. Body coiled, poised to strike, the viper's triangular head hovered just above the six-inch high dry grass. While walking a deer hunt, I'd seen the snake the same moment I'd heard its rattle—more the *ssshhhh* sound of a lawn sprinkler than the jangle of a baby's rattle that I might have expected. I stopped two paces back from the snake, slowly lifted my rifle and clicked off the safety. Adrenalin surged; my heart hammered my sternum.

Gramps' words echoed in my mind: "With a rifle, especially one with a scope, it's impossible to aim close-up at a snake. So to shoot a rattler, you gotta' make him do the aiming for you."

Following Gramps' instruction, I extended both arms, finger on the trigger, holding the rifle away from my body, not aiming through the scope, but pointing the barrel as best I could a few inches from the snake's head. Slowly, I moved the barrel three or four inches to the left, then back to the right. As Gramps had predicted, the snake alertly followed the barrel's movement with a right and then a left turn of its head. Pausing for a moment in the center, I then moved the barrel up, and then down a few inches. The rattler continued to follow my movement, like an attentive dancer following a partner's lead. Once more, I moved the barrel left—this time only an inch or two—then right an inch, then left a half-inch, then right—slowly, slowly centering my dance partner's gaze, and then stopping. The snake flicked its trident tongue momentarily, tasting the air. The deadly rattler was now staring straight up the bore of my gun barrel. Dead straight. I held my breath, squeezed the trigger, and blew the poisonous viper's head to smithereens.

Michael A. Messner

Gramps and I in Chualar Canyon (circa 1959).

I have told that story so many times I figure it must have happened. But right now, as I write, I am certain it didn't. I can conjure a clear memory of Gramps' voice as he instructed me in the art of killing a rattler in this way. And I do recall once on a deer hunt when I was about twelve walking up on a rattlesnake, its head elevated above the dry wild oats, the garden-hose hiss of its rattles warning me not to take another step. But on that occasion, it was I who danced, not the snake. My feet performed a seamless 180: one moment I was trudging directly forward, the next moment, I was on my toes boogying backwards double-time, followed shortly by a forward-marching loop that took me thirty yards around the snake and any presumed serpent-den of family members lurking in the neighborhood.

The fact that my snake-execution fable creatively melded two real memories—one, Gramps' fantastical lesson on how to face down and kill a rattler; the other, the time I turned tail and ran from a snake—is consistent I guess with my boyhood need to conjure myself at the center of heroic fantasies. Most of the imaginary stories of my childhood were private daydreams, castles in the air to which I escaped to envision myself as courageous, valiant. But my rattlesnake yarn was so delicious, I could not keep it to myself as mere fantasy. I just had to tell this story to others, and I repeated it so many times I eventually convinced myself that it really happened. It was, after all, *based* on real memories.

It makes perfect sense that it was Gramps' voice in the back of my head—not Dad's—that conspired with me to spin the rattlesnake fable. Dad was very black-and-white about right and wrong, truth and falsehood. I never heard Dad curse or take the name of the Lord in vain. When Dad was my high school coach, my teammates ribbed me that "Walrus," as they called him behind his back, was unlike any coach they'd seen. He never cussed at us, never even said "damn." I wasn't totally proud of this fact, and dubbed my Dad "Mr. Clean" around my teammates.

Dad believed that any self-respecting person would know that "If it's worth doing, it's worth doing right." And there was one right way to do any job. There was one right way to use a knife and fork at the dinner table: fork in left hand stabs the meat as knife in right hand cuts a bite-size piece; set down knife, transfer fork to right hand, lift fork to mouth and chew meat well before swallowing. I sat always just to Dad's left at the dinner table, and when I'd try to wolf a piece of meat into my mouth holding the fork in my left hand, eagle-eyed Dad would always see it and would sharply smack the back of my right hand with his own fork.

Dad had a clear and literal sense of right and wrong: certain things were true and good, like the U.S. Navy, a barbequed steak (medium rare), and college football. Other things were false and wrong, like communism, Vienna sausages, and golf. When the movie M*A*S*H came out in 1972, I saw it with friends and recommended it to Mom and Dad as the funniest movie I'd ever seen. It never occurred to me that they wouldn't like it. A few days later, after they'd seen it, Dad told me he was appalled that I had recommended it to them. It wasn't just that the movie made the U.S. Military look like a bunch of dunderheads.

"My God!" he said, "They even make fun of *football*, and—and *cheerleading!*"

Movies like M*A*S*H, I can see now, blurred Dad's sense of clarity about right and wrong, good and evil. Dad often lamented, when the topic of movies came up, "I don't know why they don't make more movies like *The Sound of Music*," a film that affirmed his conviction that there are good people in the world with good values and that they will triumph over evil.

By contrast, there were ample stretches of gray-zone in Gramps' world. Starting when I was about eight, Gramps would give me one sip of wine out of his glass near the end of every dinner. Dad didn't stop this practice, but he made it clear that he preferred I'd wait until I reached the legal age of twenty-one. When in 1962 I expected to please Gramps with my patriotic understanding of good and evil by calling Fidel Castro a "dumb bearded monkey," he scolded me:

"He's no monkey. He's a very intelligent man."

I had no idea what to say to this. I'm pretty sure up to that point I'd never heard anybody say a kind word about Communist Castro, the Number One Enemy of Freedom in the Western Hemisphere. Gramps was no communist, but he also knew that the world was a complicated place. He would have no truck with knee-jerk simplistic thinking.

Gramps could also be pretty loosy-goosy with the truth. He told mythical tales, fantastic fish stories that I realized early on I should not take as a literal description of what really had happened. Take for instance the pork chops story Gramps told about his childhood:

"My aunt put a platter of pork chops on the table," Gramps said. "There was only enough for each person to have one. But there was one pork chop left on the platter, and everybody wanted it. So my uncle said, 'We will turn off the lights, and everybody can make a stab for the last one.' When the lights came back on, my uncle had the pork chop on his fork, and seven forks stuck in his hand."

That story was told frequently at Gramps' supper table—we would actually request that he tell it—and was always followed by laughs, groans, and a smattering of applause. Gramps' stories were funny, but they also were more than simple entertainment. As I grew older, I came to think of Gramps' stories as parables or allegories intended to communicate some deeper moral meaning. To a boy like me who always had access to seconds at the dinner table—or thirds if I wanted, and then mounds of ice cream and cake for dessert—the pork chops tale was simultaneously unbelievable, funny, and instructive. The story contrasted the cornucopia of daily abundance enjoyed by our family with Gramps' childhood of scarcity. It also, I think, hinted at a theme important to Gramps: the centrality of the Man of the House, the family patriarch who is willing to pay the price of leadership, and thus deserves to get the last pork chop.

Other of Gramps' tall tales were similarly fabricated, but their meanings were harder to interpret. They seemed to mask some mystery or perhaps some personal wound too deep for him to convey literally. Once, as I sat with Gramps at his desk, he slipped off his ring and told me to go ahead and try it on. This was not the first or the last time Gramps would lend me the ring for a few minutes, as though we were both rehearsing the ring's future. As I twirled the Black Hills gold ring that hung loosely on my skinny ring finger, I imagined it years in the future, snug on my full-grown hand.

"You know," Gramps said, dropping into his quiet, sing-songy storytelling voice, "Your dad and I used to go hunting sometimes over on Fred Jacobs' property. One time there, I sat down for a smoke on the side of a hill, and I lost the ring. Looked and looked, and couldn't find it. Figured it was lost forever. The next year, we went back there to hunt with Fred, and I sat down in the same place, put my hand on the ground, and the ring just slipped right back on my finger."

I looked down at the ring on my finger, doubting, but wanting to believe: "Really?"

"Yep. Just slipped right back on my finger. A year later."

That evening, alone with Dad, I repeated this story and asked him if it was true. He laughed, "Gramps likes to tell stories," he said simply.

Michael A. Messner

My eighth birthday with Granny, and Gramps displaying his ring (1960).

I had a hard time swallowing that one. And whereas I *get* the pork chops story, I'm not sure I understand the ring story, what it's supposed to mean. I doubt its literal factuality. But I know that there must be an emotional truth to this tall tale of the ring hiding in the dirt on a wild hillside for a full year, patiently waiting for its owner's return, then miraculously slipping back on to Gramps' hand. Magical properties or no, there's no getting around that there was something special about that ring to Gramps. In several photos I have of him, he appears consciously to be displaying his left hand, as though the ring is the principal subject of the picture.

Gramps was more than simply proud of that gold ring set with the Lake Superior agate stone. J. P. Kelly's ring and its companion pistol held some deep meaning to Gramps, and they are supposed mean a great deal to me. I'm pretty sure that the fact that Gramps inherited the ring and the revolver from his Uncle John, who raised young Russell as though he was his son, is the key. The ring was a tangible connection to the man who was the closest thing to a father that Gramps would ever have. And since I was his only grandson, the ring would naturally go to me, as a right of primogeniture. The way Gramps made such a point of telling me stories about the ring, implying its magical powers as it dangled loosely from my skinny finger, implied that he saw the ring as an extension of himself, to a future me.

Gramps imagined that this future me would spawn more future Messners. Once, about a year before he died, as I followed him around the house doing laps behind his walker, he paused and asked with sudden fury, "When are you going to give me a great-grandson?"

I understood what Gramps was driving at. He was telling me that I was responsible for replicating his Messner name through the male line. Ignoring the patrilineal implications of Gramps' plea, I played dumb and innocently referenced my sister's reproductive success: "You already have two great-grandsons through Terry—Eric and Adam."

Gramps erupted, staggering a bit as he took his right hand off his walker to shake his fist at me. "I mean a *Messner!*"

Both hands back on the walker, pausing for a breath—"*Huh-Huh*"—he calmed himself. "How old are you?"

"I'm twenty-eight."

"Look. I don't know what's gonna' happen to the house after I'm gone. You get yourself married, I'll give you the whole dump."

It's not that Dad never told a lie. After all, when I was thirteen years old he'd let me in on a subterfuge that he and Gramps had deployed to pull the wool over the eyes of the women in our family.

In my backyard cabaña today, I have three sets of deer antlers that Gramps mounted vertically on a narrow plank of varnished wood in 1965. These antlers meant the world to Gramps. He displayed them together because this was the only year that each of us—me, at the age of thirteen, Dad at forty-five, and Gramps at sixty-eight—shot a buck. Dad's, mounted on top, is a respectable rack for a California Coastal deer. The one on the bottom, Gramps' buck, has a pathetically tiny seven-inch spread. And the middle one—my buck—is an asymmetrical spread; the left side had once had a fork, one prong of which was neatly broken off at its base. I imagined my buck had snapped his antler off in some heroic battle with another buck, or maybe a mountain lion. Probably he just broke it off on a tree, when his antlers were young, soft and itchy. Any way you look at them, none of these antlers shout "trophy" at you. But Gramps lovingly mounted them, and they hung together on the wall of his cabaña as a proud reminder of a kind of Messner hunting trifecta. But Gramps knew—and I do too—that those three mounted antlers meant far more than that.

A couple of weeks into this 1965 season, I got my buck on "the Olive Trees" hunt. Halfway up the mountain, we spotted two deer, way up near the top. Dad and Bob examined them with their binoculars, whispered to us that the second one had horns with at least a fork on one side—a legal buck. Bob's son Duffy and I fired away from long distance: me with my .300 Savage, Duffy with his 30-30 popgun. The deer stumbled, as though hit, and went on. Dad and Bob pursued it while Duffy and I waited behind. Half an hour later, we heard a single shot. They had found the buck already wounded, they later told us, and they were not sure who hit it, Duffy or me. For some reason, they decided the deer was mine. I accepted the credit, but doubted whether I really hit it.

Dad and Gramps got their two deer a few weekends later. Dad got his on Saturday morning; Gramps got his on Sunday morning on a typical group hunt that had been neatly planned out, military-style, the previous night after dinner. As dawn was breaking, Gramps dropped us off at the top of a canyon. He then drove the jeep back down the hill and sat himself at the bottom of the canyon to wait and watch, as the rest of us worked our way down the brushy ridges and rocky bottom, hoping to funnel a buck toward Gramps.

King of the Wild Suburb

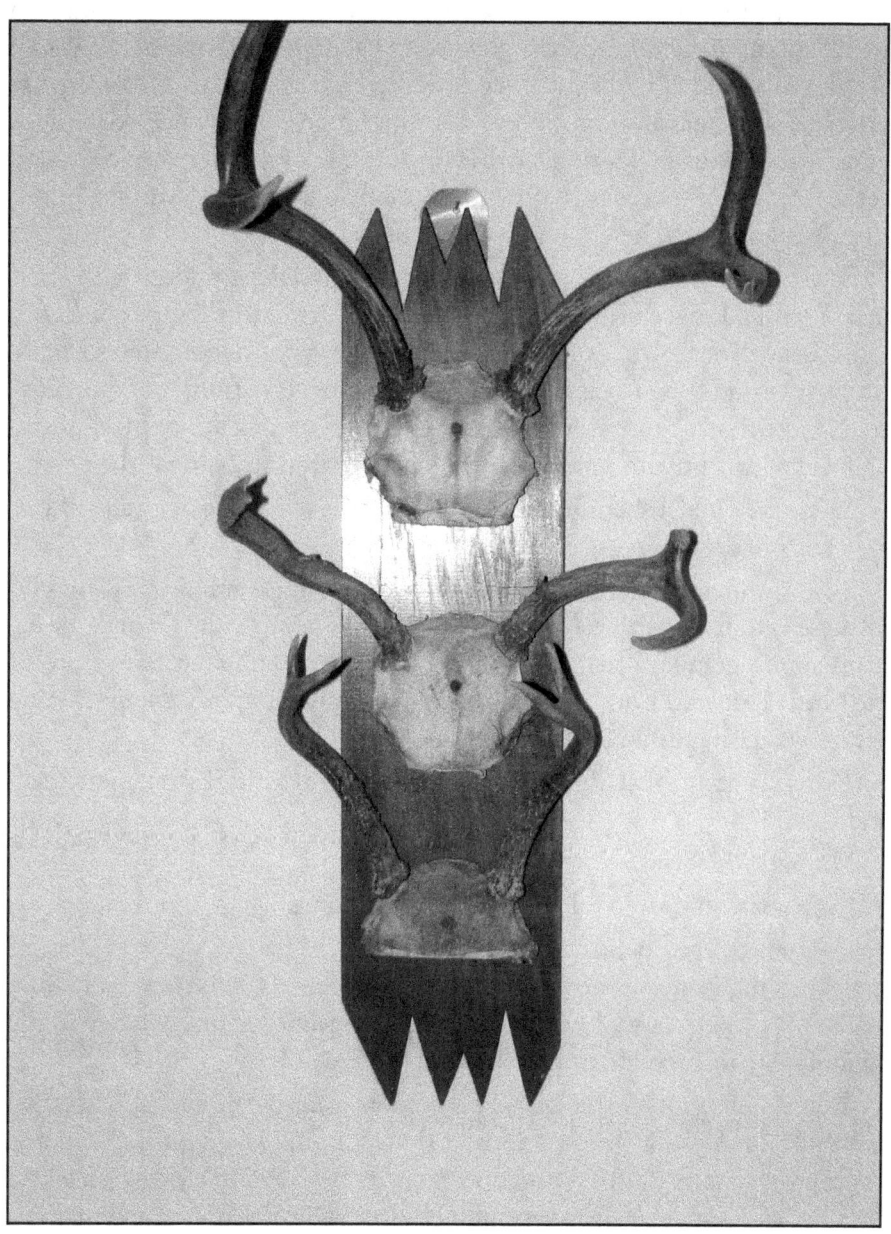

The 1965 Trifecta symbolizes a secret conspiracy among the Messner men.

As he waited, Gramps engaged in his usual careful ritual. First, he would walk a ways down from the jeep, find the perfect vantage point, and smooth out a flat seat in the dirt, with a good solid backrest. Before long, he'd pull out his pack of Old Gold's and have a smoke; he'd follow this with a Pep-O-Mint lifesaver. Year after year, a Pep-O-Mint lifesaver surely helped Gramps get through hours of waiting, sitting on the side of a hill, his rifle cradled in his lap. Sometimes, despite the lifesaver, he'd doze a bit. And somehow, on this day in 1965, he ended up with a buck.

Later, back at the cabin, Dad and Gramps posed for photos with their deer. I recalled that during the hunt, our group had been spread apart, so I hadn't seen Gramps shoot his deer. And in fact it was hard for me to figure out how he had done it, given his location. I asked questions, but didn't get much more than a grunt from Gramps. Finally, Dad took me by the arm and walked me to a private spot under the oak tree that stood near the cabin.

"Son," he said, "I shot Gramps' deer. In fact, I've shot *all* of Gramps' deer for the past several years."

I was stunned to silence. I immediately reran in my mind the scenes I'd witnessed annually, with each triumphant arrival home with "Gramps' deer," as my mom, grandmother, sisters and I oohed and ahhed at the return of the Great Hunters. Dad was letting me in on a big, important manly code here, a secret handshake.

"There are some things, Pal that we don't tell the women. You understand?"

I nodded my head.

"Someday, son," he said, "I hope you can do the same for me."

This was the sort of lie that Dad would willingly participate in. He made it clear to me how important this secret was. And to this day, Dad's final words—"Someday, son, I hope you can do the same for me"—lodge in my memory like a barbed foxtail poking through my sock.

When I mentioned this story to my mom a few years ago, she laughed and said "Oh, don't you think I knew that? Granny knew it too." It turns out, I guess, that I was the only one back then who didn't know that Dad was shooting Gramps' deer for him. This was a broader-based fabrication than I had imagined at the time. Everybody was in on this conspiracy of silence, the collective aim of which was to prop up the image of the aging family patriarch.

Even during his heyday, it was clear that Gramps was a paper lion, a patriarch with lots of bark and little bite. Granny was the strong one, and pretty much everybody knew Gramps needed her to prop him up. When somebody remarked on some other man's admirable physical strength or muscular prowess, Granny could be relied upon to note the fact that Gramps' "barrel chest" was most impressive. On cue, before she could even get this declaration fully on the table, Gramps would noticeably inhale through his nostrils, his chest indeed barreling. Granny almost literally inflated Gramps, right before our very eyes. Never was this more apparent than in the months and years after she slipped and fell in a Safeway store, breaking her hip. She was in her early seventies at the time, and still very vibrant. But after the fall, a series of physical problems beset her. She began to forget things, and gradually descended into a confused dementia. With his buttress eroding, it wasn't long before Gramps began to sway noticeably too.

By the time I moved in with them, a year after my Dad's death, Granny was largely bedridden, disoriented and skinny as a rail. My aunt employed a daytime caretaker, a sturdy middle-aged African American woman named Mayberry Lovejoy, who came to the house at 7 a.m. sharp and stayed through 3 p.m., Monday through Friday. Mayberry was good at what she did. She was warm and caring but could also be tough as nails in the face of Gramps' frequent bursts of anger. Mayberry and I became a kind of tag-team on weekdays: I'd head off to the university in the mornings, and if I'd return home after 3:00, Mayberry would have left a hot dinner sitting on the stove for me to serve.

Weekends though, could be tough. If I wanted to go out somewhere, I'd have to first be sure that Granny and Gramps had eaten their breakfast that they'd each washed down their daily medley of meds and that Granny had had a successful visit to the "potty chair" that sat next to her hospital bed in the living room. One Saturday afternoon, I stayed too long at a party with other graduate students. I enjoyed myself drinking beer, smoking dope and laughing with my friends. When I opened the door of Granny and Gramps' house at 5:30 p.m., I entered a different world. If two old people could create pandemonium, this was it.

Granny was wandering around the house. I found her in the kitchen, propped on her cane, calling out "Daddy—whoo-hoo!—where are you Dad?"

Gramps was lying on the dining room floor, jammed between a chair and the pedestal base of the table. As I approached him, he started yelling at me: "God damn it, Mike! Where the hell have you been?"

I yanked myself as best I could out of my pleasant party stupor. I walked Granny back to her bed and tucked her in, trying to reassure her that Gramps

Following Dad's death, Granny's and Gramps' health and spirits plummeted (1977).

was okay. Then, I went back to the dining room and knelt on both knees next to Gramps.

"Are you okay? Are you hurt? Is it your hip again?"

His anger had dissipated; he was now sheepish: "I—I shit myself."

Sure enough, he reeked. I got him up and to the bathroom, gave him a sponge bath and fresh clothes, and then got him to bed. After that day, I would not again leave them alone on a weekend for more time than it would take to make a short trip to the grocery store. My friend Bill Solomon frequently came over on a Friday or Saturday night, shared dinner with us, and then stood sentry with me in my room, both of us getting high and listening to music late into the night. Some weekends, Linny or Terry would drive up from Salinas and help out. Monday mornings at 7:00 a.m., when I heard the metallic clack of Mayberry Lovejoy's key opening the front door, I felt like the U.S. Cavalry had arrived.

Granny suffered from a series of ailments, including painful shingles that covered the left side of her torso. Though Mayberry and I tended to her as best we could, Granny would be in and out of the hospital during the two years I spent with her and Gramps. Once, after a dispiriting visit to Granny in the hospital, as I veered Gramps and me off the freeway ramp and on to Claremont Avenue, we passed the Safeway store where Granny had suffered her fateful fall.

"Curse you!" Gramps said as he shook his fist in the direction of the store. "That's where it all started," he said. "Those bums said she just fell on her own. I know she slipped on something." As we rolled up Claremont Avenue, he added once more for good measure: "Curse you!"

Those days—his son dead, Granny slipping away from him, his own health deteriorating—Gramps seemed at a loss. I tried to get him to watch his once-beloved Oakland A's with me on TV, but after a couple of innings, he'd announce he was tired and drag himself off to bed. He'd pretty much lost interest in watching anything on television. The daily *Oakland Tribune* that Mayberry or I would set next to his place at the table every morning would remain there, unopened. He almost never went into his cherished back yard garden, nor could he climb the stairs to visit his den. Gramps' world was shrinking, closing in on him. His continual silence was punctuated by bursts of exasperated fury, directed at Mayberry or me. He became noticeably nervous, anxious, uncertain of what to do next. Once when Granny was in the hospital, as he and I sat eating dinner, Gramps dropped his fork with a sudden clank on his plate, and displayed his right hand, trembling in a way that seemed to me purposely exaggerated.

"Look at me," he said. "I'm shaking like a leaf."

I asked if there was something I could do.

"Nope. There's nothing," he said. Suddenly he was sobbing, "I just think about my Momma laying there."

Gramps was shrinking. His ring had started slipping unpredictably off his hand, and we'd have to search for it in his bed or on the carpet. Finally one day he unceremoniously took the ring off and handed to me.

"Keep it," he said.

I clutched its familiar warmth in my hand, not slipping it on my finger, not yet. "Are you sure?"

"Yep. If I hold on to it, I'm gonna' lose it."

A couple of times, at Gramps' request, I would rub his aching shoulders and neck with baby oil as he sat slumped forward in his dining room chair.

"Aahhh. God. That feels good. Thank you."

I was repulsed by the gross tactility of my slick oily hands on the bumpy skin of Gramps' back, and would only massage him when he asked me to. After he died, I remembered these few grudging backrubs as the only times that I was certain that I was bringing Gramps some relief, and I bludgeoned myself with private, mournful guilt that I'd not done it more often, willingly.

Once, during these final days, as we sat for a moment after dinner and Gramps was in a somewhat more buoyant mood than usual, I popped the question I'd been wanting to ask, "Are you afraid to die?"

"No. No, I'm not afraid to die."

He didn't elaborate, but it seemed true that he wasn't afraid to die. It was the sad uncertainty of living these final days that was so terrible for him—not knowing exactly what would come next, but knowing for certain that Granny—his "Momma"—was not going to get better.

The last time Gramps went to the hospital was just after Christmas in 1980, for a nasty flare-up of what he called his "breathing trouble." He'd developed emphysema a few years back, and had actually stopped smoking. When he was a younger man, Gramps had bragged, "You can't tell me that smoking causes cancer. I started smoking when I was twelve, and I don't have cancer." As a very little kid, I remember hearing him each morning in his bathroom, noisily hawking up nasty hunks of phlegm as he cleared the passageways for another day of Old Gold smokes. Now, he no longer smoked, but he was prone to flare-ups of his "breathing trouble" that left him gasping and wheezing. A plastic breathing exercise device he'd brought home from his last hospital stay sat at his place at the table, on the very spot his ashtray used to rest.

Gramps was in and out of the hospital several times during the time I lived with him—once for the broken hip, the other times for his "breathing trouble." Each previous time, he'd rallied to get himself better, doing the breathing exercises hourly, rebuilding his leg muscles after the hip surgery, doing what he had to do to get home again. This time, January 11, 1981, the last time I saw him alive, Gramps no longer had that desire.

"C'mon, Gramps, you gotta' do the exercises so you can get home. Maybe a week or two, okay?"

"Nope. Not this time," he said. "I'm done."

I wouldn't accept that. Or maybe I didn't believe that he really meant it. He was, after all, prone to almost childish attention-seeking theatrics. "No, Gramps, you can do it. You've done it before."

He just shook his head.

Two days later, on my return home from a seminar, I got the call from my aunt, who was in tears. Gramps had died in his sleep, she told me.

The day after Gramps died, I visited Granny, who had been in a convalescent hospital for the past several weeks. I was determined to tell her about Gramps' death, in hopes that she too would let go. She was asleep when I arrived, but a gentle touch awoke her.

"Hi there," she said sweetly through her toothless mouth, most likely not knowing who I was.

"Hi, Granny, it's Mike."

"Oh. Oh, Mike. Where's Daddy?"

I took her hand in mine. "Granny, Gramps died yesterday. He died very peacefully, in his sleep."

"Oh, my," she said, her milky eyes suddenly riveted to mine, her fingers digging into my hand with surprising strength. "Oh my, my." She began to cry and I did too. We sat silently for a minute or two.

"Granny, you remember how you used to tell me about your grandmother and grandfather who died on the same day? You always said that was the most wonderful thing, for them both to go to heaven together on the same day. Do you remember that?"

"Yes," she said through her tears. "Yes, I think so."

"Maybe—I thought—maybe you could go too, today, with Gramps to heaven?"

"Oh, my yes, that would be wonderful, wouldn't it?"

I held her hand as she dozed off, and then I left. A few days later I returned to visit her and she asked me again, "Where's Dad?" Determined, I dragged her once again into the pool of grief, telling her of Gramps' death and reminding her of her grandparents' miraculous near-simultaneous natural deaths. But after each visit—after each time she'd doze off, even—she would forget this, and the next time she'd ask again where her Daddy was. So I decided no longer to put us both through this. Subsequently, I'd tell her the comforting lie that "Gramps is fine; he sends his love."

My visits to Granny became less and less frequent. When I'd drop in on her, she was always asleep in her bed, thinly cadaverous, rice-paper-thin translucent skin over bone. Still, she retained a determined set to her jaw, as though she patiently awaited one more visit from her Daddy. Some steely girder inside Granny stubbornly sustained her, keeping her breathing for nearly three more years.

○

I sat in the aisle seat on the familiar hard wooden pew of Bethlehem Lutheran Church in Berkeley. Linny, Terry, and Mom sat silently to my left. It seemed so recent that we'd been in a church together like this, burying Dad. I remembered sitting in this same pew as a young boy next to Dad, and how he'd reach over with his strong hand, firmly squeezing my thigh one, two, three times, sending ripples of ticklish pleasure through my whole body, making me shiver, and keeping me from nodding off during the sermon.

On this day of Gramps' funeral in 1981, the organ prelude had ended, and Pastor Teachenor's voice echoed in the silent church as he read the opening Lesson from the Book of Revelations. I reached into my pocket. At first I thought I'd forgotten them, but then my fingers found the hard cylinder. I pulled out the fresh pack of Pep-O-Mint Lifesavers, peeled it open, and offered one to Linny. She smiled, took one, and passed them on to Terry.

Later, after the funeral, Linny told me, "The Lifesavers: Nice touch, Mikey. But your timing was off—too early. Gramps would have waited until the sermon, when the boredom had set in."

Within a few weeks, I moved to a run-down house in Berkeley's flatlands. It was apparent that Granny would never come home from the hospital. I'd not yet married—much less produced more Messner boys—so I had not qualified under Gramps' rules of primogeniture to receive his offer to give me "the whole dump." My mom, aunt and uncle decided to sell the house at 5905 Claremont Avenue to Pastor Teachenor. With deep feelings of grief, I cleared out of the beloved family home—leaving behind objects, artifacts and spaces that formed a tangible foundation for memories of my childhood, of Dad, Granny and Gramps. I could not bring with me Gramps' beautiful garden or his spectacular den. But with the help of several friends, I took Granny's gas stove and some of her kitchen utensils. I packed off to my new home with Gramps' mission gun cabinet, complete with all of its mysterious treasures. And I took Gramps' oak desk, on which I now rest my hands as I write tall tales about rattlesnakes, pork chops and magic rings.

Epilogue: Hunting for Each Other

June 17, 2009

Dear Miles and Sasha:

Tomorrow is a day I have anticipated for over thirty years. I will wake up in the morning having lived one day longer than my dad, who died thirteen days shy of his 57th birthday.

You guys probably won't remember this: When you were very young, and I was leaving for a few days for an academic conference, I'd come to each of your bedrooms early in the morning to kiss your warm cheek, and whisper in your ear, "Always remember that your dad loves you." My greatest fear then was that I'd die suddenly—a plane crash, a massive heart attack in a distant hotel—and you'd be left with no clear memory of me.

My father's death in 1977 stands out as the singular emotional watershed event of my life. It was that moment, at the age of 25, when I had just begun to inch back toward my father, having spent my late teens and early twenties wrenching myself away from him. This was the most confusing and fraught time in my life, as I sought to define myself in opposition to my father, while also knowing on some deep level that I loved and admired him.

Dad's death left me feeling emotionally ripped off, my barely-begun process of reconciliation incomplete. God, my father would have loved your mom, and I'd have loved for the two of you to know him. I've so often wished that my dad had lived long enough to see me get my adult act together—finishing my Ph.D., getting a professor job, marrying and having you kids. For many years, the people around me have intuited this need. My mom, my sister, even my dad's surviving friends, seem never to miss an opportunity to tell me, "Daddy would be so proud of you."

Nearly two decades ago, I was invited to speak to a church group about the meaning of fatherhood on the occasion of Father's Day. At the time, I was a novice dad. Miles, you were a toddler, barely walking and talking; and Sasha, you were still but a gleam in your mom's eye. But I stood in front of a group of fifty people of varying ages and assumed the role of expert on fatherhood.

The punch-line to my talk was this: too many men immerse themselves for years in their public lives, separating themselves from their families, only to wake suddenly one day with a sick realization: "My kids have grown up. I wasn't there for them when they were little. I missed the boat with them, and now it's too late." As I scanned the room, my eyes rested on a frail old man, sitting in a wheelchair at the back of the room. He was quietly weeping. I felt for him, and imagined family wreckage scattered in the wake of his life. But I also confess that I felt smug in my own certainty: I will never be that old man. I will never have that kind of regret. I will always be connected with my kids.

Nearly twenty years of fathering has left me feeling less sanguine and way more humble about making any claims of success, much less expertise, as a father. Father-son relations are, if anything, more mysterious to me than ever.

I still wonder, what does a son get from his father, and how does he get it? Gramps, who didn't grow up with a father, gave his name—both his first and last—to my father. He also gave him a hunting rifle, a dog and his companionship in the California mountains. My father was often absent from my daily life, busy as he was with his admirable public life. Against the unlit backdrop of his absence, the rare moments I had with Dad still shine like emotional beacons in my memory: a drive to Candlestick Park for a Giants game; a shootaround, just the two of us, at the high school gym; and of course, two or three hunting trips with Gramps each year.

So now I wonder, what have I given you guys? And here's an unsettling truth: I always told myself that my own sons would not need emotionally salient memories like hunting trips with their father—and they most certainly would not need guns—because their father was always around, a constant presence in their lives. Do you remember years ago, when I first showed you guys my slide show on deer hunting and shared with you the story of the emotional trauma of my first kill? Afterwards, Miles asked immediately, "So, when are we going hunting?" I laughed, taking it as at least a half-joke. But

I silently wondered, will I ever be able to do something with my sons that will replicate the memorable salience of hunting with my dad? At the time, I believed that it was not needed. I figured that somehow you guys would just soak up by osmosis my love, my life lessons and progressive values, just by being in the same general vicinity with me as I washed dishes, folded laundry, wrote books and e-mail in my home office, and just hung around the house.

In retrospect, that sounds inadequate to me. Writing this memoir has helped me to zero in on the fact that during those rare moments in the past with my father and grandfather, I learned deep and enduring things about life. I learned how to set goals and meet them. I learned how men—even when they don't openly talk about it—demonstrate care for each other. I learned how those hunting trips with Dad and Gramps were actually about fathers and sons finding a way to love each other. These outings were not so much about hunting for deer: they were about hunting for each other.

And maybe that's the crux of it. If there is some essence to a father-son relationship, maybe it's about a mutual search for each other. Perhaps the tensions built into the unequal relationship of authority between father and son, along with the bumpy dynamics of adolescent boys' and young men's cascading emotional development all together create a kind of puzzle, a set of mysteries to be worked through over a lifetime.

Looking at it this way, I feel hopeful. On this day when I know, finally, that I have out-lived my father, that I will have at least one more day, perhaps even many years, I wonder what I may still offer to you. In this moment, I feel I'm pausing briefly, having climbed barely halfway up a very steep mountain, gazing up at the distant summit, hunting for you. One thing I learned while hunting with Dad is to take such a climb a step at a time, focusing not on the apparently unreachable top of the mountain, but on the small rock or shrub twenty paces away. And then the next one.

Another thing I know, and I learned this mostly from Gramps: I can offer you the gift of my stories. I give you this memoir in hopes you will connect with the stories of my grandfather, my dad, and me. I pass on to you the emotional truths and the mysteries of these stories. Sasha, Miles, take my stories, ponder them and make what you will of them as you forge the stories of your own lives.

And by all means, keep the ring and the gun together.

Love,
Dad

Author's Note

The stories in these pages stirred in my mind for years, but the serious writing began during the winter of 2008 when I joined a memoir class taught by Mona Gable at Vroman's Bookstore in Pasadena, California. There I met four fellow memoirists, and together we formed a writing group that continues today. Sherry Breskin, Natalie Cousins-Robledo, Elizabeth McNamara Salvinksi and Susan Hoffman read and commented on every piece in this book—usually more than once. It is not possible to overstate how important Sherry, Nat, Liz and Susan have been to the development of this book. They are four talented writers, skillful editors and encouraging friends who helped me to believe in the merit of my work.

Several generous friends read parts or all of the manuscript. Thanks to Bob Blauner, Jim Clark, Hiram Davis, Donnie Hallstone, Pierrette Hondagneu-Sotelo, James Jasper, Maureen Parton, Pam Roby, Jon Scattini and Christine Williams for helpful suggestions and advice on earlier drafts. Vicki Forman provided professional editing for the final revision of the manuscript. Jon Miller, Sally Pratt, Walter Irish, and Jan Dizard aided me in filling in details about German, Russian, cars and deer hunting. Betsy Amster, Mitch Sisskind, and Michelle Nordon gave me valuable advice about the publishing world. I extend oodles of thanks to Blue Trimarchi, who contributed invaluable technical advice and generous assistance on photo preparation. I am grateful to the late Susan Bright, the visionary leader of Plain View Press, and to Pam Knight, who shepherded my book through the production process. I am proud to have my book join the list of such a progressive press.

It requires ongoing emotional support to sustain the labor that goes in to a work of the heart. Friends Laurie Narro and Oscar Narro buoyed me over the long haul. As I drafted the stories that make up this book, I sent each piece to my mom Anita Messner-Voth, my sister Melinda Messner-Rios, and my niece Samantha Rios. Mom, Linny and Sam never failed to respond to my yarns with loving words of encouragement. My partner for almost three decades Pierrette Hondagneu-Sotelo and my sons Miles Hondagneu-Messner and Sasha Hondagneu-Messner also rooted me on—and whenever I asked, they listened patiently as I read aloud the few pages I had just written.

Dad and Gramps—the two main characters in this book—are no longer with us. The process of remembering and writing has made me feel closer than ever with them, and with Granny too. My sister Terry whose own memory was cruelly stolen from her and from us by Alzheimers disease, would have loved to share the memories in this book, I am certain. Fred A. Raab, my grandfather on my mom's side, was the skillful shutterbug who shot many of the photos that appear in these pages. It is my hope that this book provides a small link from those people and their worlds, to those of us still living, that we might hunt together for a more peaceful tomorrow.

About the Author

Michael A. Messner was born in Salinas, California, and educated from kindergarten to Ph.D. in California's once-great public schools. Since 1987 he has worked as a professor of sociology and gender studies at the University of Southern California. The author of several books, he teaches and speaks publicly on issues of gender-based violence, the lives of men and boys, and gender and sports. He lives in South Pasadena with sociologist and author Pierrette Hondagneu-Sotelo. They are proud of their two sons Miles and Sasha. *King of the Wild Suburb* is Mike's first published memoir.

www.ingramcontent.com/pod-product-compliance
Lightning Source LLC
Chambersburg PA
CBHW052050070526
44584CB00017B/2112